# THE VEGETARIAN TABLE

## THAILAND

# THE VEGETARIAN TABLE

## THAILAND

## JACKI PASSMORE

PHOTOGRAPHY BY STEVEN ROTHFELD

CHRONICLE BOOKS · SAN FRANCISCO

# DEDICATION

To Isobel, daughter, friend, and critic, who can't pass a day without tofu.

Text copyright © 1997 by Jacki Passmore.
Photographs copyright © 1997 by Steven Rothfeld.

Library of Congress Cataloging-in-Publication Data:
The vegetarian table: Thailand/by Jacki Passmore.
p. cm.
Includes index.
ISBN 0-8118-1214-6 (hc)
1. Vegetarian cookery.  2. Cookery, Thai. I. Title.
TX837.P326 1997
641.5'636'09593—DC21   96-51123
CIP

Book Design: Louise Fili Ltd.
Design Assistant: Tonya Hudson
Food Styling: Victoria Roberts-Russell
Food Styling Assistant: Michele Repine
Prop Styling: Carol Hacker
Carol Hacker wishes to thank the following for their generosity:
Indo Arts, San Francisco
Ethnio Arts, Berkeley
Chao Thai Restaurant, San Anselmo

Photograph on page 2: Vegetables in Hot Orange Curry Soup, page 75.

Printed in Hong Kong.

Distributed in Canada by Raincoast Books
8680 Cambie St., Vancouver, B.C. V6P 6M9

10 9 8 7 6 5 4 3 2 1

Chronicle Books
85 Second Street
San Francisco, CA 94105
Web Site: www.chronbooks.com

# CONTENTS

◈

# INTRODUCTION

**V**EGETARIANISM IS AN ANCIENT TRADITION IN THAILAND, WHERE SAFFRON ROBES AND BUDDHIST TEMPLES COLOR THE LANDSCAPE, AND THE PEOPLE ENJOY A VARIED DIET OF DELICIOUS DISHES BASED ON LEGUMES AND SOYBEAN PRODUCTS, AND NATIVE AND INTRODUCED VEGETABLES. They gather spinachlike water vegetables from the banks of their *klongs* (waterways) and *paddies* (flooded rice fields), and edible leaves like the betel, *bai champluu.* They grow the unique frilly, ribbed winged bean and yard-long green beans. They cultivate a plethora of eggplants, some as tiny as peas, and Chinese cabbages of many varieties. They plant corn and potatoes, pumpkin and melons, and have a native supply of edible fungus, bamboo, lotus, and water chestnuts from their mountains and wetlands.

Nature itself provides plenty to eat, so Thai cuisine, in principle, follows the Buddhist precepts on the slaughter of animals, evolving with a moderate use of red meat. Beef butchers are most often Pathans from the north, descendants of seminomadic tribes that originated in present-day Pakistan and Afghanistan, while the pork and poultry butchers are Chinese. Hunting is generally regarded with contempt.

But seafood is different. The catch from the sea and from inland rivers and waterways has been an important nutritive source in the Thai diet for centuries. It offered an affordable food, if Thais cared to help themselves, while meat was more expensive, and its protein equivalents could be satisfactorily obtained from tofu and other soybean products. Several significant sauces and seasonings that are key elements in traditional Thai cooking are made from seafood, in particular fish sauce (*nam pla*), shrimp paste (*kapi*), and dried shrimp (*gung haeng*). They bring to Thai food the uniquely pungent aromas and deep essential flavors that are its signature.

Thus, centuries ago, the Buddhist Thais proposed a charming rationale for the inclusion of some seafood in their diet: If a fish is stupid enough to swim into a trap and die, then we may as well eat it! Many Thai vegetarians choose to overlook the use of traditional seafood-based seasonings, curry pastes, sauces, and relishes in their cooking regime, while others prefer to adhere to a strict diet that uses only vegetable-derived seasonings.

## THE FLAVORS OF THAILAND

I relish the pungent, herbaceous flavors that are unique to Thai cooking, and have been determined to achieve them in these recipes while devising toally vegetarian alternatives to the many seafood-based pantry staples. I found, for example, that the simple replacement of fish sauce with soy sauce was not the best alternative. It subtly changed the nature of the dish, giving it a taste more akin to Chinese food. In Chapter One under The Essentials, I offer my solution to the total exclusion of seafood-based products in Thai cooking. Under the heading The Vegetarian Alternative, I have listed several significant vegetarian seasoning ingredients, or combinations of ingredients, to replace standard nonvegetarian products. My vegetarian curry pastes, sauces, and relishes, included in the section Curry Pastes, Sauces, Stocks, and Garnishes, are all suitable for the complete vegetarian diet.

I have relied heavily on tofu (bean curd) as a meat substitute, and have made minimal use of eggs. When the latter do appear in a recipe, they can often be omitted, and I have indicated so. I have attempted to use only ingredients that are readily available from supermarkets or most Asian food suppliers, and preceding the Glossary, which explains the Thai and Asian ingredients used in the book, you will find a short list of ingredients that should be present in your Thai pantry.

## THE BASICS

Thai cooking is quick and easy, and you don't need to purchase any special equipment. I will, though, take this opportunity to praise the practicality of the Chinese wok as a brilliantly versatile cooking pan, and the perfect pan for deep frying. Many of these recipes have been double tested in a standard cooking pot and in the latest acquisition for my kitchen, a high-heat electric wok with a superlative nonstick interior and a tight-fitting lid. The latter allows me to cook with notably less oil, a consideration that many will appreciate.

On the subject of oils, and therefore of health, I have used peanut oil in the majority of these recipes, for no more reason than the Thais have a fondness for peanuts, enjoying their nutty flavor. Any of the good vegetable oils, or monounsaturated oils like canola or light, flavorless olive oil, can be substituted. If you are working with a good nonstick pan, reduce the amount of oil, as required. The section The Essentials offers random notes on preparation and cooking methods, and a word on chilies and onions.

## EATING THE THAI WAY

About the only time people in Thailand eat a single dish is when they are having a quick bowl of noodles or a one-plate meal of cooked food on rice. At mealtimes, the table becomes a fiesta of flavors and colors, with several dishes served at once to eat with plain white or flavored rice.

I have tried to achieve a compromise between Thai tradition and lifestyles beyond Thailand's borders, just as is done in most Thai restaurants outside the country. Therefore, the soups, starters, snacks, and salads that might normally be brought to the table as an integral part of the collective meal can be served as first courses. Serving amounts are noted on each recipe.

In giving yields for main courses, I have assumed portion sizes based on one main dish with an accompaniment of rice. If more than one main course or curry is offered, or if a vegetable side dish or noodle dish accompanies the main dish, the meal would serve more than the number advised on the main course recipe.

Thai food is a visual and taste treat, and none of its majesty is diminished in this collection of vegetarian recipes. *Gan gin gan yuu*—"As you eat, so you are."

CHAPTER ONE

THE

ESSENTIALS

# THE ESSENTIALS

APPROACHING A NEW CUISINE IS ALWAYS EASIER WITH AN UNDERSTANDING OF THE COOKING PROCE-
DURES AND BASIC PRINCIPLES OF SEASONING. Equally important is a knowledge of how the food is served. Thai food, even the most humble meal, can be a flamboyant display of artistry, color, and flavor. The first impression is of the table. In restaurants and homes, food is served with ornately worked silver spoons from gleaming silver tureens onto decorative blue-and-white porcelain. Even if the silver is merely aluminum, it is highly polished, rendering it as impressive as the real thing. Serving dishes are raised on pedestals, so they grace the table with distinction. Formal meals are set out on individual low, round tables called *kantokes*. Even at roadside stalls or backstreet cafes, you may eat from handcrafted ceramic bowls or baskets intricately woven from strips of banana leaf.

Next is the food itself. In Thailand every dish is presented for maximum visual appeal. Rice and noodles are mounded high in a bowl, and dishes are lavished with fresh herbs, draped with delicate shreds of golden egg crêpe, or crowned with a tangle of finely shredded red chili or scallion greens. Vegetables and fruits are never just sliced, but carved elaborately to decorate platters, serve with dips, or to finish the meal. Desserts and sweet snacks are brightly colored with edible food dyes. The tantalizing fragrances that announce the arrival of a Thai meal awaken new senses, mesmerizing diners before they even begin to eat.

In The Vegetarian Alternative, I explain the essential flavor elements. Since Thai cooks traditionally make extensive use of seafood-based seasoning ingredients, this section gives vegetarian replacements, including substitutes for important ingredients to suit the vegan. The various cutting, slicing, chopping, and shredding methods employed in the Thai kitchen are discussed in the section Notes on Preparation and Cooking Methods, along with instructions for grinding spices.

On Chilies and Onions answers the vexing question of which chilies and onions to use, and how to identify them. Curry Pastes, Sauces, Stocks, and Garnishes gives recipes and formulas used throughout these pages, to provide authentic Thai flavors and finished dishes. Your Thai Pantry offers a list of cooking essentials that can be kept on hand in your pantry, refrigerator or freezer; and the Glossary gives an explanation of all of the Thai or Asian ingredients used in these recipes, along with details on how to identify, use, and store them.

# THE VEGETARIAN ALTERNATIVE

COMMERCIALLY PRODUCED **THAI CURRY PASTES** INVARIABLY INCLUDE SHRIMP PASTE, FISH SAUCE, AND DRIED SHRIMP OR FISH IN THEIR INGREDIENTS. The many *dipping sauces, dressings,* and *relishes* that accompany Thai dishes are often based on seafood products as well, such as shrimp paste, or dried shrimp ground to a floss. In the recipes in this book, I have listed vegetarian sauces and seasonings along with their standard nonvegetarian alternatives where appropriate. I have devised special recipe formulas for vegetarian versions of classic Thai sauces and seasonings, which can be found beginning on page 14. Following is an explanation of how I have chosen to replace four seafood seasoning ingredients, fish sauce, oyster sauce, shrimp paste, and dried shrimp, with vegetarian alternatives.

Fish sauce (*nam pla*), a thin, amber-colored, salty sauce, is the predominant seasoning sauce used in Thai cooking. In Thai vegetarian cooking, fish sauce is usually substituted by a light (thin) soy sauce, which, as I have already noted, results in a taste more akin to Chinese than Thai cuisine. I have opted for a minimal use of soy sauce, adding additional salt and/or the brine and solids of two vegetarian ingredients, salted yellow beans (more commonly known as yellow bean sauce), and fermented tofu (bean curd), a pungent product of cubed tofu pickled in brine, sometimes with chili added.

To appease both the vegan who eschews all animal products, including milk and eggs, and the less restricted vegetarian who consumes certain fish and shellfish, I have given the common seafood-based ingredient and its totally vegetarian substitute. For example, an ingredient line might read "¼ cup fish sauce, or 1 tablespoon light soy sauce and 1 tablespoon mashed yellow bean sauce." Another example might read "2 tablespoons fish sauce, or 1 tablespoon light soy sauce and salt to taste." Therefore, the fish sauce in the first example would be substituted with *both* the soy sauce *and* the yellow bean sauce, which together impart the flavor required for the particular recipe, while the fish sauce in the second example would be substituted with a lesser amount of soy sauce (so the soy flavor and color do not intrude into the dish), with salt added to taste.

Oyster sauce (*nam man hoy*) is used in some Thai dishes. It is a rich, thick brown sauce made from fermented dried oysters. A Malaysian product, *sos chendawan*, is a 100 percent vegetarian version made from mushrooms and vegetable protein. It is labeled vegetarian mushroom oyster sauce, and can be used in any recipe as a vegetarian substitute for oyster sauce.

Shrimp paste (*kapi*) is a salt-fermented shrimp product used extensively in Thai cooking to give the food its characteristic deep and vibrant flavors. *Kapi* comes in two forms, fresh and dried. The former is a soft, rose-pink paste, quite salty, and sweetly pungent. It is sold in jars and is best kept in the refrigerator. Dried shrimp paste is more concentrated in flavor and aroma. It is a gray-pink color, has a dryer, firmer texture, and is sold in sticks wrapped like butter, or packed into jars. They are interchangeable in recipes, unless specifically noted. Chinese shrimp sauce or Malaysian *blacan* can be substituted. Simply excluding it in vegetarian cooking results in bland and uninteresting tastes. I use various salt-fermented soybean products such as yellow bean sauce, Chinese bean pastes, fermented tofu (bean curd) in brine, and tempeh.

Dried shrimp (*goong haeng*) has been replaced by a variety of bean products, roasted nuts, or coconut.

GRINDING: Thai cuisine calls for few elaborate cooking procedures, although many traditional dishes often required tedious and intricate procedures in times when labor-saving appliances were not available. Today, the painstaking pounding of spices and herbs for curry pastes, powders, and relishes that was previously done in a wooden or stone mortar can be achieved in a blender, spice grinder, or in a small food processor. Many Thai chefs, however, still cling to old methods, claiming they achieve a superior result from hand pounding their ingredients. I admit I often prefer the large granite mortar and pestle in my kitchen to my electric-powered grinding appliances.

STIR-FRYING AND DEEP FRYING: Stir-frying, in the Chinese tradition, is used in Thailand. It entails using a wok over the highest heat possible, and keeping the contents of the pan in constant motion by turning, stirring, and mixing with a spade-shaped spatula. A wok is also invaluable for deep frying, as its wide, curved sides help to ensure hot oil does not boil over. But remember, for safety, your wok must be securely positioned over your gas heat source, on a stand specially made to accommodate the pan. Use a wok with a flat bottom if you cook on an electric stove.

COOKING CURRY PASTES: Curry pastes must be cooked thoroughly to release their full flavor potential. The most common practice is to fry them briefly over medium heat with a little oil while stirring constantly, and then to add some of the liquid from the dish, in many instances coconut cream, and simmer the paste in the liquid. This will take from 5 to 15 minutes, and the coconut cream will thicken and reduce in that time. In the case of red curry sauces, the curry base is ready for the addition of the other ingredients only when a slick of red oil floats on top of the coconut cream.

CUTTING INGREDIENTS: The recipes include many different terms for cutting ingredients, which are explained here. *Mincing* is very, very fine chopping that is best achieved by slicing the ingredient very thin, then using a large, heavy knife or Chinese cleaver to chop or mince the slices until you have pieces about the size of sesame seeds. *Chopping* is a coarser version of mincing, and results in pieces somewhere between the size of a peppercorn and a pea, depending on the ingredient. *Coarse chopping* refers to cutting pieces into chunks of a size suitable for grinding in a blender or food processor. *Grating*, usually used in reference to fresh ginger, should be done on the fine perforations of a hand-held grater. *Very fine slicing* requires slices so thin that the knife blade can almost be seen through them. The direction applies in particular to lemongrass, which is quite woody and would be inedible if not properly cut. *Shredding* refers to fine slivers, more slender than a matchstick, while *matchstick* pieces are the size of their namesake. Both are best achieved by first slicing to the required thickness, then stacking the slices and cutting across them to the appropriate fineness.

CHILIES: Not all Thai food is hot, but Thais do appreciate the fiery qualities of the chili. In all recipes, I have made allowance for personal preference in the amount of chili used. Five types of chili are commonly used in Thai cooking. Bird's eyes (their Thai name, *prik khee nu suan*, translates as "rat droppings") are tiny red, green, or yellow chilies that are viciously hot. More commonly available are *prik khee nu*, which are 1 to 1½ inches long, red or green, and very hot. Next come *prik chee faa*, medium-sized red or green chilies that are slightly less hot. *Prik yuak* are large and a pale yellow-green. Mild in comparison to the others, they can be used for stuffing and in salads. *Prik haeng* are large red chilies, usually sold dried, very hot, and a deep red-brown color.

**Chili flakes** are dried red chilies with their seeds, ground coarsely into flakes. **Ground dried chili**, sometimes called **chili powder**, is finely ground, seeded dried red chilies. **Roasted chili powder**, made by dry-roasting chilies with spices, is frequently used in Thai cooking as a dressing and condiment and is easily made: Heat a small, heavy saucepan or skillet over medium-high heat, without oil. Add 1 tablespoon hot ground dried chili, ¼ teaspoon salt, and ¼ teaspoon ground coriander. Heat for about 1 minute, stirring slowly and continuously to avoid burning the powder. Remove from the heat and let cool. Transfer to a spice jar to store. Keeps for several months in a tightly capped jar. **Roasted chili paste** is the same recipe cooked with vinegar and a little oil: While the mixture is still in the pan, reduce the heat to medium-low, add 1¼ teaspoons distilled white vinegar and 1½ teaspoons vegetable oil, and heat, stirring continuously, for about 2 minutes. It is used as a seasoning, for which an unroasted chili sauce or paste could be substituted.

*Thai chili sauces* vary enormously, from sweet, clear, and viscous to thick, smooth, scarlet and incendiary. Where *chili paste* is called for in a recipe, I have tended to suggest the Indonesian *sambal ulek* for two reasons. Firstly, it has a fine flavor that is both hot and rich, and secondly, it is a product that is generally available. You can make you own chili paste by grinding fresh red chilies to a paste, using salt as the abrasive. It will keep for only about 24 hours in the refrigerator. *Sambal ulek* and other chili pastes should be refrigerated, and if not used often are best preserved by pouring a thin film of flavorless vegetable oil over the surface to prevent oxidation. Thai chili flakes, powders, pastes, and sauces are usually made with hot chilies, so approach with caution.

ONIONS: Thai cooks use onions generously. Common yellow and red salad onions, scallions (also known as green onions) and leeks are all important in the cuisine, but it is their smaller, red or gold-skinned cousin, the shallot, that is favored. About the size of a large garlic clove, the shallot has a delicate taste that is particularly appealing. If unobtainable, use small yellow onions or the alternative suggested in the recipes.

Crisp-Fried Shallots (page 24) are used in cooking and garnishing Thai dishes.

# CURRY PASTES, SAUCES, STOCKS, AND GARNISHES

## RED CURRY PASTE

MAKES ABOUT ¾ CUP

THIS VEGETARIAN RED CURRY PASTE, KNOWN AS **KRUNG GAENG PED**, IS REASONABLY HOT, SO IN THE RECIPES I HAVE ALLOWED SOME LATITUDE IN THE HEAT YOU CHOOSE FOR YOUR DISH. KEEP IN MIND, THOUGH, THAT THE CURRY PASTE IS THE ESSENTIAL FLAVOR ELEMENT, SO A TOO-CAUTIOUS ADDITION WILL MEAN A LESS FLAVORFUL FINISH. IF YOU PREFER YOUR THAI FOOD ON THE MILD SIDE, DECREASE THE AMOUNT OF CHILIES USED IN THIS PASTE.

2 tablespoons coriander seeds

½ teaspoon fennel seeds

2 teaspoons black peppercorns

1½ teaspoons dried shrimp paste, or 1 tablespoon mashed yellow bean sauce

4 to 5 tablespoons peanut or vegetable oil

1 lemongrass stalk, trimmed and coarsely chopped

5 lime zest strips

1 small yellow onion, coarsely chopped

3 large fresh coriander (cilantro) roots

5 thick slices fresh galangal or ginger, peeled

4 large, hot fresh red chilies, or 10 Thai prik khee nu red chilies, seeded

6 large garlic cloves

2 teaspoons Crisp-Fried Shallots (page 24)

2 teaspoons sweet paprika

1 teaspoon salt

In a wok or skillet without oil, combine the coriander and fennel seeds and the black peppercorns and dry-roast over medium heat, stirring frequently, until fragrant, about 4 minutes. Transfer to a spice grinder or mortar and grind to a fine powder. Sift through a fine-mesh sieve to remove large particles, and set aside.

If using the shrimp paste, in the same pan fry the paste in 1 tablespoon of the oil over medium heat for about 40 seconds, stirring and mashing it against the side of the pan. It should be very aromatic. Remove from the heat and set aside.

In the spice grinder or mortar or in a blender, grind together the lemongrass, lime zest, onion, fresh coriander, galangal or ginger, chilies, and garlic until reduced to a paste. Add the fried shallots and grind again until smooth. It may be necessary to add some of the oil, to help emulsify the ingredients.

Heat the remaining oil in the wok or skillet over medium-high heat and add the lemongrass mixture. Stir for about 3 minutes, then add the ground spices, the shrimp paste or yellow bean sauce, the paprika, and the salt. Reduce the heat to medium and fry for about 5 minutes, stirring the curry paste constantly so it cooks evenly. It should be a deep red-brown color and very aromatic. Remove from the heat and let cool completely.

Transfer to a sterilized jar and, to prevent oxidation, smooth the top of the curry paste and cover with a film of oil. Cap tightly and store in the refrigerator for up to several weeks.

# MUSSAMAN CURRY PASTE

MAKES ABOUT ½ CUP

**M**USSAMAN IS A RELATIVELY MILD CURRY PASTE, BUT IF YOU PREFER TO PLAY IT SAFE, USE ONLY 1 CHILI WHEN YOU MAKE UP THIS RECIPE.

In a small saucepan, skillet, or wok without oil, combine the coriander and cumin seeds and dry-roast over medium-low heat, stirring frequently, until fragrant, about 3 minutes. transfer to a spice grinder or mortar and grind to a fine powder with the cloves and peppercorns. set aside.

Add the oil to the pan and place over medium heat. When hot, add the onion or shallots and fry, stirring often, until lightly browned, about 3½ minutes. Add the garlic, ginger, and lemongrass and fry, stirring frequently, until browned, about 1½ minutes. Drain the chilies, add to the pan, and fry for a minute or so, then stir in the salt.

Transfer the contents of the pan to the spice grinder or mortar and grind to a paste. Let cool completely. Transfer to a sterilized jar and, to prevent oxidation, smooth the top of the curry paste and cover with a film of oil. Cap tightly and store in the refrigerator for up to several weeks.

*2 tablespoons coriander seeds*

*2 teaspoons cumin seeds*

*2 whole cloves*

*4 black peppercorns*

*1½ tablespoons peanut or vegetable oil*

*¼ cup finely chopped yellow onion or shallots*

*1 tablespoon minced garlic*

*2 teaspoons minced or grated fresh ginger*

*1½ tablespoons minced fresh lemongrass*

*2 dried red chilies, seeded and soaked in hot water to cover for 15 minutes*

*1 teaspoon salt*

# VEGETARIAN NAM PRIK POW SAUCE

MAKES ABOUT ¾ CUP

**N**AM PRIK POW IS ADDED TO SALADS AND VEGETABLE DISHES TO IMPART A TYPICAL HOT-SWEET-SOUR FLAVOR, AND CAN ALSO BE SERVED WITH A MEAL AS A CONDIMENT. IN THE NONVEGETARIAN THAI CUISINE, **NAM PRIK POW** IS SOMETIMES CALLED **TOM YAM** SAUCE, AS IT IS THE FLAVOR BASE FOR THE FAMOUS SOUR-AND-HOT THAI SHRIMP SOUP, **TOM YUM GUNG**. THE HOT AND SOUR SOUP WITH BEAN THREAD VERMICELLI, TOMATO, AND BASIL ON PAGE 69 ALSO CALLS FOR THIS POTENT SAUCE.

*1 cup peanut or peanut oil*

*½ cup chopped garlic*

*½ cup chopped shallots or yellow onion*

*½ cup seeded and chopped dried red chilies*

*4 teaspoons yellow bean sauce*

*1½ tablespoons vegetarian mushroom oyster sauce*

*1½ tablespoons light palm sugar or superfine white sugar*

In a wok or skillet, heat the oil over medium to high heat, and add the garlic. Fry the garlic to a rich golden brown, stirring it constantly in the oil, about 3 minutes. If it becomes too brown, the garlic develops an acrid taste and will have to be discarded, so watch it carefully. When it is ready, using a slotted spoon, transfer it to a plate. It is not necessary to drain the fried garlic on paper towels, as it will be returned to the oil after grinding.

Fry the shallots or onion in the same way for about 4 minutes, then remove to the plate. Repeat with the chilies, frying them for about 1 minute, until browned. Once the chilies have been removed from the oil, pour off half the oil from the pan. Set the pan aside.

Place the chilies, garlic, and shallots or onion in a mortar, spice grinder, or blender and pound or grind to a paste. Add the bean sauce and work to a smooth, firm paste. Return the paste to the oil in the pan, and stir in the oyster sauce and sugar.

Place over low heat and cook, stirring continuously, for 2 to 3 minutes, then remove from the heat and let cool completely. Transfer to a sterilized jar, cap tightly, and store in the refrigerator for up to several months.

NOTE: It is essential that the garlic, shallots or onion, and chilies be fried separately, as they brown at different rates. For a nonvegetarian version of this seasoning, use 1½ to 2 teaspoons dried shrimp paste, dry-roasted for 1 minute in a wok or skillet, in place of the yellow bean sauce and vegetarian oyster sauce.

# VEGETARIAN NAM JIM SAUCE

MAKES ABOUT 5 TABLESPOONS

**N**AM JIM IS A SALTY SAUCE OR DRESSING USED FOR TART SALADS WHEN A HOT AND SALTY FLAVOR IS REQUIRED, SUCH AS FOR THE GREEN PAPAYA SALAD ON PAGE 80. IT COMPLEMENTS SALADS COMPOSED OF FRESH, CRISP FRUIT AND SUCH CRUNCHY SALAD VEGETABLES AS RADISHES, BEAN SPROUTS, JICAMA AND WATER CHESTNUTS.

Place the chilies, coriander root, and garlic in a mortar or spice grinder and pound or grind them to a coarse paste. Add the soy sauce, lime or lemon juice, sugar, and salt and continue to pound or grind until well mixed. The sauce does not have to be too smooth. Dilute with the cooled water, mixing in well. Transfer to a nonmetal container, cap tightly, and store in the refrigerator for up to 1 week.

1 to 2 large, mild fresh red chilies, seeded

2 small, hot fresh red chilies (optional)

1½ teaspoons chopped fresh coriander (cilantro) root

1 or 2 large garlic cloves

2 teaspoons light soy sauce

2 tablespoons freshly squeezed lime or lemon juice

2 teaspoons light palm sugar or superfine white sugar

1 teaspoon salt

1 tablespoon boiling water, cooled

# SWEET CHILI SAUCE

Serve this smooth sauce with its mild hint of chili with "fish" cakes (page 46), golden spring rolls (page 50), and fried tofu with three sauces (page 55).

½ cup distilled white vinegar

¾ cup superfine white sugar

1 teaspoon minced garlic

1 teaspoon sambal ulek *or other chili paste*

½ cup water

1 tablespoon cornstarch

Combine all the ingredients in a small saucepan, stir well, and bring to a boil. Reduce the heat to medium-low and simmer, stirring, for 2 minutes. Remove from the heat and let cool completely. Transfer to a sterilized jar, cap tightly, and store in the refrigerator for up to 1 month.

# CHILI RELISH

MAKES ABOUT 1½ CUPS

CHILI RELISH ADDS PEP AND FIRE TO ANY OF YOUR FAVORITE DISHES. IT IS ON THE HOTTER END OF THE CHILI SCALE, SO IF YOU ENJOY FLAVOR WITHOUT EXCESSIVE HEAT, DECREASE THE AMOUNT OF CHILI FLAKES USED IN THE RECIPE.

In a nonstick or stainless-steel saucepan over medium-low heat, heat the oil. When hot, add the onions and garlic and cook, stirring occasionally, for about 15 minutes. Add the chili flakes and cook, stirring, for a few seconds, then add the tamarind concentrate or lemon juice, sugar, ¼ cup of the water, and the salt. Cook over medium-low heat, simmering until the relish is thick and caramelized, about 12 minutes.

In a small dish, stir together the cornstarch and the remaining ¾ cup water. Pour into the pan, and increase the heat to medium-high. Cook, stirring continuously, until the relish is translucent and thickened to the consistency of a thin conserve, about 3 minutes. Check for taste—it should be sweet, hot, sour, and salty—and adjust as needed.

Remove from the heat and let cool completely. Transfer to a sterilized jar, cap tightly, and store in the refrigerator for up to several weeks.

*½ cup peanut oil*

*1 cup finely chopped yellow onions*

*5 teaspoons minced garlic*

*2 tablespoons chili flakes*

*1 tablespoon tamarind concentrate, or 2 tablespoons freshly squeezed lemon juice*

*½ cup medium-light palm sugar or soft brown sugar*

*1 cup water*

*1 teaspoon salt*

*2 teaspoons cornstarch*

# PEANUT SAUCE

MAKES ABOUT 1 CUP

**S**ERVE THIS CREAMY, MILDLY SPICED SAUCE WITH GRILLED OR DEEP-FRIED TOFU (BEAN CURD), OR AS A DRESSING OVER COOKED VEGETABLES.

*1 lemongrass stalk, trimmed and coarsely chopped*

*1 thin slice fresh galangal or ginger, peeled*

*1 large garlic clove*

*2 red shallots, or ⅓ small yellow onion, peeled*

*1 or 2 small, hot, fresh red chilies*

*1 tablespoon peanut or vegetable oil*

*1 tablespoon fish sauce or light soy sauce*

*2 teaspoons medium-light palm sugar or soft brown sugar*

*1 teaspoon tamarind concentrate, or 2 to 3 teaspoons freshly squeezed lemon juice*

*4 to 5 tablespoons smooth or chunky peanut butter*

*1 cup coconut milk, or ½ cup coconut cream and ½ to ¾ cup water*

*Salt and pepper to taste*

*1 tablespoon finely chopped fresh coriander (cilantro) leaves (optional)*

Place the lemongrass, galangal or ginger, garlic, shallots or onion, and chili in a spice grinder or mortar and grind or pound to a coarse paste.

In a small nonstick pan over medium heat, warm the oil. Add the ground ingredients and fry, stirring frequently, until lightly browned, about 5 minutes.

Add the fish or soy sauce, the sugar, tamarind or lemon juice, and the peanut butter. Add half of the coconut milk, or diluted coconut cream and stir with a wooden spoon until the mixture is well blended. Slowly add the remaining liquid to make a sauce of pouring consistency.

Season to taste with salt and pepper and cook, stirring continuously, for about 1 minute. Stir in the coriander, remove from the heat, and let cool before using. The sauce can be stored in a covered container in the refrigerator for up to 3 days.

# CUCUMBER VINEGAR SAUCE

MAKES ABOUT 1½ CUPS

THIS CLASSIC DIPPING SAUCE IS A PERFECT ACCOMPANIMENT TO MANY THAI SNACKS, ESPECIALLY FRIED OR ROASTED FOODS.

In a small saucepan over medium heat, combine the vinegar, sugar, and *sambal ulek* or other chili paste and heat gently. Remove from the heat and pour into a bowl to cool to room temperature.

Stir the coriander and cucumber into the cooled sauce and serve immediately, or transfer to a tightly capped container and store in the refrigerator for up to 4 days.

*1 cup distilled white vinegar*

*6 tablespoons superfine white sugar*

*1 to 3 teaspoons sambal ulek or other chili paste*

*1 tablespoon finely chopped fresh coriander (cilantro)*

*2 tablespoons peeled and finely chopped cucumber*

# WHITE VEGETABLE STOCK

USE THIS STOCK IN SAUCES, SOUPS, AND DISHES WHERE A DELICATE FLAVOR AND LIGHT COLOR ARE REQUIRED. VEGETABLE STOCK CAN BE KEPT FOR ABOUT 5 DAYS IN THE REFRIGERATOR, OR FROZEN FOR UP TO 3 MONTHS.

*Stems from 2 bunches fresh coriander*
*(cilantro)*
*Stems from 1 bunch fresh basil*
*12 thin slices fresh ginger*
*2 large garlic cloves, halved*
*2 scallions, white parts only*
*2 cups (9 ounces) peeled and cubed*
*Japanese white radish*
*2 cups (9 ounces) peeled and cubed*
*chayote or Chinese melon*
*3 quarts water*

Combine all the ingredients in a soup pot. Bring barely to a boil, then reduce the heat to low and simmer gently for about 20 minutes. Strain through a fine-mesh sieve into containers, let cool, cap tightly, and refrigerate or freeze.

# DARK VEGETABLE STOCK

MAKES 3 TO 4 QUARTS

USE THIS STOCK WHEN A DEEP COLOR AND STRONG, SMOKY FLAVORS WILL ENHANCE THE RECIPE. IT CAN BE KEPT FOR UP TO 5 DAYS IN THE REFRIGERATOR, OR FROZEN FOR UP TO 2 MONTHS.

Preheat an oven to 400 degrees F. Place the onions, shallots (if using), garlic, tomatoes, carrot and pumpkin in a large, heavy pan suitable for the oven. Place in the oven and roast, turning the vegetables at least once during cooking, until the vegetables are well darkened on some surfaces, about 55 minutes.

Transfer the pan to the stove top and add the radish, the coriander and basil stems, the ginger, and the water. Bring barely to a boil, then reduce the heat to low and simmer uncovered without allowing the water to bubble, for about 20 minutes. The stock should be deeply colored and very aromatic.

Strain through a fine-mesh sieve into containers. Let cool, cap tightly, and refrigerate or freeze.

2 yellow onions, unpeeled, quartered

8 shallots, unpeeled (optional)

5 garlic cloves, unpeeled

2 tomatoes, quartered

1 carrot, peeled and chopped

2 cups (9 ounces) peeled and cubed
    pumpkin

2 cups (9 ounces) peeled and cubed
    Japanese white radish

Stems of 1 bunch fresh coriander
    (cilantro)

Stems of 1 bunch sweet basil

10 thin slices fresh ginger

3 to 4 quarts water

# CRISP·FRIED GARLIC OR SHALLOTS

IN THAILAND, COOKS LIBERALLY SPRINKLE FRIED GARLIC OR SHALLOTS OVER ALL KINDS OF COOKED DISHES AND SALADS. THEY ADD SOME NUTRITIONAL VALUE AND A PLEASANT CRUNCH. IN SOME INSTANCES, AS IN THE RECIPE FOR "FISH" CAKES ON PAGE 46, THESE GOLDEN BROWN SLIVERS ARE USED AS AN INGREDIENT TO CONTRIBUTE COLOR AND FLAVOR, RATHER THAN AS A GARNISH. THESE PANTRY STAPLES CAN BE PURCHASED READY-MADE FROM ASIAN STORES, BUT ARE NOT AT ALL DIFFICULT TO MAKE AT HOME, AND WILL KEEP FOR MONTHS AWAY FROM MOISTURE AND HEAT.

*1 head of garlic, or 8 to 12 shallots*
*¾ cup corn, light olive or vegetable oil*

Peel the garlic or shallots and, using a small, sharp knife, thinly slice them lengthwise, keeping the slices uniform. If the garlic slices are large, turn them flat on the board and cut them into fine slivers.

In a small saucepan over medium-high heat, heat the oil. When hot but not smoking, add the garlic or shallots (do not attempt to cook both at the same time, as their cooking times may vary). Cook, stirring from time to time, until the pieces are a good golden brown, retrieving them from the oil with a slotted spoon before they begin to darken. Cooking time will be 4 to 5 minutes. If they are overcooked, they will acquire a bitter taste. Place on paper towels to drain and cool. Pat with paper towels to remove any surface oil. When completely cooled they should be quite crisp and dry. Pack into a small covered jar or a lock-top plastic bag.

NOTE: The frying oil is deliciously flavored with garlic or shallot. Filter it and save for stir-frying, or to add to deep-frying oil for extra flavor. It will keep for about 10 days.

# GARNISHING

THAI COOKS PRIDE THEMSELVES ON THE VISUAL ARTISTRY OF THEIR FOOD, AND MANY OF THEM HAP-
PILY WHITTLE AWAY FOR HOURS ON VEGETABLES OR FRUITS, transforming them into elaborate ornamental pieces for the table. On an everyday basis, food is rarely served without some embellishment, whether it be a single frond of coriander (cilantro), a few pieces of cucumber skin carved to resemble green leaves (a Thai favorite), or "flowers" made from red and green chilies. An egg crêpe, scallions, chilies, and leeks are cut into fine, long shreds to drape over rice, noodles, or curries, and tiny carrot "blossoms" adorn stir-fries. Crunchy edible garnishes such as fried garlic and shallots (page 24), chopped roasted peanuts, or potent roasted chili powder (page 13) are also popular. Even rice is used, toasted and ground to fine granules, to add textural interest and additional flavor to a finished dish (see Vegetarian Laab, page 81).

TO MAKE CHILI FLOWERS, select smooth-skinned fresh chilies. Using a small, sharp knife, cut them into strips, working from the shoulder to the tip, but do not sever them at the shoulder end. Trim away any internal fibers that cling to the strips, then place the whole chili in a dish of ice water. After about 30 minutes, the "petals" will have curled out-
ward to make elegant flower shapes. They can be kept in a glass container in the refrigerator for about 5 days.

TO MAKE CURLED CHILI SHREDS, select smooth-skinned fresh chilies. Using a small, sharp knife, cut them in half lengthwise and scrape out the seeds and internal fibers. Cut into long, fine shreds. To curl them, place in a dish of ice water for about 30 minutes. To keep, fold a clean kitchen cloth and moisten it. Place in the bottom of a plastic container, put the chili curls on top, cover, and keep in the refrigerator for about 5 days.

TO MAKE SCALLION CURLS, cut the green parts of scallions lengthwise into narrow strips, and place in ice water to curl. Shavings cut from a large carrot can be handled in the same way.

TO MAKE CUCUMBER LEAVES, use a small, sharp knife to cut ovals from the skin of a cucumber and trim to a point at both ends, one end tapering more than the other. Using the small, sharp knife or a carving tool, remove narrow strips of the green in a formation that resembles the veins on a leaf. These, too, will last for several days in the refrigerator.

# YOUR THAI PANTRY

**B**Y MAINTAINING A BASIC STOCK OF THESE THAI INGREDIENTS IN YOUR PANTRY, REFRIGERATOR, AND FREEZER, YOU CAN PREPARE DELICIOUS VEGETARIAN THAI MEALS with a minimum of advance planning. Dried ingredients will keep for many months in the pantry. Fresh products can be stored in the refrigerator for up to 3 weeks, and frozen goods in the freezer for many months.

Black Fungus (pantry)

Chili Bean Paste (pantry)

Coconut Cream (pantry/freezer)

Curry Pastes (refrigerator)

Dried Chilies (pantry/freezer)

Dried Shrimp (refrigerator)

Fermented Tofu (pantry)

Fish Sauce, if diet permits (pantry)

Fried Tofu (bean curd) (refrigerator/freezer)

Galangal (refrigerator/freezer)

Garlic (pantry)

Ginger (refrigerator)

Hoisin Sauce (refrigerator)

Jasmine Rice (pantry)

Kaffir Lime Leaves (refrigerator/freezer)

Lemongrass (refrigerator/freezer)

Limes (refrigerator)

Mushrooms, canned and dried (pantry)

Noodles, various (pantry)

Palm Sugar, light, medium-light, and dark (pantry)

*Sambal Ulek* (refrigerator)

Shrimp Paste, if diet permits (pantry)

Soy Sauce, light and dark (pantry)

Tamarind Concentrate (pantry)

Vegetarian Mushroom Oyster Sauce (refrigerator)

Yellow Bean Sauce (pantry)

# GLOSSARY

ABALONE MUSHROOMS: See mushrooms.

BASIL: In a cuisine where herbs are a strong feature, basil is the star. Thai cooks use a wide variety of basils, lavishing them into curries and sauces, garnishing with them, or tossing them into salads. Common sweet basil is fine to use, but investigate your Asian food markets for alternatives. Look for purple, holy, basil-mint, hairy.

BEAN CURD: See tofu.

BEAN SPROUTS: Fresh bean sprouts are used extensively in Thai cooking. Rinse before use and drain well. Store in a sealed plastic bag in the refrigerator for up to 3 days. Canned bean sprouts should be drained and soaked in ice water to reinstate some of their crispness.

BLACK FUNGUS: This crinkly, gray-black edible fungus is also known as wood ear or tree ear fungus for its peculiar earlike shape. Sold fresh or dried in whole pieces or shreds, the dried fungus should be soaked to rehydrate, which triples its volume. It is an excellent vegetarian product that is easily obtained in Asian food stores. Fresh black fungus should be kept in the vegetable crisper of the refrigerator for up to 1 week, while dried black fungus keeps indefinitely in dry conditions. White fungus is more delicate in texture and taste, but can be used instead of the black. It is sold dried and in cans.

BLACK MUSHROOMS: See mushrooms.

BOK CHOY: See Chinese cabbages.

CHILI BEAN PASTE: This pungent seasoning sauce combines ground or crushed fermented soybeans, ground red chilies, and garlic with salt and soy sauce. Powerfully flavored and often intensely hot, it is sold in jars and, once opened, should be stored in the refrigerator where it will keep for many months. Yellow bean sauce mixed with chili paste is a successful replacement.

CHILIES: See The Essentials, page 13.

CHILI OIL: An infusion of chilies in vegetable oil, this hot condiment is useful when a hint of chili is required in a dish or sauce. Substitute a hot chili sauce, used with discretion.

CHILI PASTE: See *sambal ulek*.

CHINESE CABBAGES: In these recipes any of the different varieties of Chinese cabbages or kale could be used. The large, tightly packed napa or celery cabbage has a mild flavor and superb texture, as does the smaller bok choy, with its round, green leaves and fleshy white stems. Choose the freshest of what is available where you shop.

CHINESE LONG BEANS: These long, slender green beans are also known as snake beans or yard beans, as they can reach at least a yard in length. The lighter green beans have marginally less flavor than the deeper green variety. Readily available, they keep for up to a week in the refrigerator and can be replaced by young green beans.

CHINESE MELON: There are several types of green or white-fleshed melons suitable for Thai cooking. They vary from small, oval, green-skinned melons to the giant winter melon. Zucchini or chayote can replace them in a recipe.

CHINESE RED VINEGAR: A distilled rice vinegar, amber-red in color, used as a condiment and in sauces. Replace with cider or brown vinegar.

CILANTRO: See coriander.

COCONUT CREAM AND COCONUT MILK: The first, thick extraction of creamy coconut liquid made by grinding fresh coconut flesh with water to achieve a smooth liquid is coconut cream. It has the consistency of heavy cream. Coconut milk is the second, thinner extraction of liquid from the same ground coconut flesh, or is coconut cream diluted with extra water. Both can be made at home in a heavy-duty blender or food processor, but canned products are more convenient and are usually of good quality. In general, coconut cream is required in recipes in which it will be reduced, or where a thick, rich, creamy sauce or dressing is required. Coconut milk is suited to soups and thinner sauces. Most canned coconut products are labeled as coconut milk, although certain brands are thick enough to suit the purpose of coconut cream. The thick coconut solids separate from the water in any can, however, so you can obtain coconut cream by opening a can of coconut milk without shaking it and simply scooping off the layer of cream that has risen to the top, leaving below a thin, clear liquid. Then, mix in as much of the thinner liquid as is needed to achieve the desired consistency.

CORIANDER: The fresh herb coriander is also known as cilantro, Chinese parsley, or *pak chee* in Thai. You simply can't cook Thai food without it, as the whole plant, and even occasionally the seed spice, is used. The leaves, whole, in sprigs, or chopped, are a garnish and ingredient in curry pastes and sauces. The stems are used in stocks and curry pastes and the cream-colored roots are an ingredient in many curry pastes and seasonings. It keeps for a few days, loosely wrapped in paper in the vegetable crisper, and is tricky to grow at home, so seek out a reliable supplier of this important herb.

CURRY PASTE: See The Essentials, page 11 and 12.

DRIED SHRIMP: See The Essentials, page 11.

EGGPLANTS: There are more varieties of eggplant grown in Thailand than anywhere else in the world. Long and slender green, white, and purple eggplants can be used in most recipes that call for the large purple variety, and vice versa. The smaller ones are unique, however. Walnut-sized white, green, yellow, or mottled purple eggplants (*makhua khun*) are eaten raw in salads, and are a feature in the vegetable platters that accompany pungent Thai dips as a first course. Even smaller are the pea eggplants (*makhua puang*), which are added to curries. They are fun to use, if available, but can be left out of a dish without ill effect, or be replaced by peas. See also Vegetarian Jungle Curry (page 102).

FERMENTED TOFU (BEAN CURD): Cubes of fresh tofu are pickled in brine, sometimes with mashed chili, and left to ferment until the tofu acquires a soft texture and salty pungency that can best be likened to an extremely aged marinated feta cheese. It is a useful seasoning ingredient, which comes into its own in vegetarian cooking. See also The Essentials, page 11.

FISH SAUCE: See The Essentials, page 11.

GALANGAL: This rhizome is such a valued seasoning in Thai cooking that they call it Thai ginger, or *kha*. It is a relative of ginger, and can be distinguished from root ginger by its tan color and its straight, thick, pink-tinged stems. If galangal is available fresh, it is peeled before use, and should be stored in the vegetable crisper of the refrigerator. Dried galangal is sold as chips and powder, and has a more peppery taste. It is sometimes sold frozen, in which case it can be sliced straight into a dish. If galangal cannot be obtained, use young fresh ginger.

GARLIC CHIVES: Identify these at the greengrocer by their slender, flat, deep green leaves and their distinct garlic fragrance. Substitute scallion greens. To store, wrap loosely in a cloth and place in the vegetable crisper for up to 1 week.

GINGER: Fresh ginger root is what is called for in Thai cooking, never dried or ground. Mature ginger has a slightly wrinkled appearance and a stronger taste, and should be peeled before use. Young ginger is a buff-colored root with a smooth appearance and cream-colored flesh. It is milder in taste and does not need to be peeled before use. Store ginger in the vegetable crisper of your refrigerator, where it will stay fresh for many weeks.

GOLDEN MUSHROOMS: See mushrooms.

GREEN PEPPERCORNS: Green peppercorns are fresh pepper berries, sold on the stem, and ready to add straight to a dish after rinsing in cold water. Pickled green peppercorns packed in brine can be used, after draining and rinsing, in any recipe calling for fresh. Store the latter in the refrigerator for up to several months.

HOISIN SAUCE: This sweet, thick brown sauce is a useful addition to your pantry. Use it as an ingredient, dip, marinade, or glaze for grills. It keeps for many months.

JAPANESE PEAR: The *nashi*, or Japanese apple-pear, is in taste and appearance like a cross between an apple and a pear. Unlike an apple, it does not go brown when cut, but remains crisp and white. Japanese pears give an appetizing crunch to salads. An unripe pear can be substituted.

JAPANESE WHITE RADISH: This large, white, tapering vegetable, also known as *daikon*, has the peppery taste characteristic of the common radish and crisp flesh. Large red radishes or Chinese green radishes can replace Japanese radishes in a recipe, but may be slightly more pungent. They will keep for weeks in the vegetable crisper of the refrigerator.

KAFFIR LIME LEAVES: These unique leaves, which grow in pairs, one above the other on the stem, have a remarkably intense citrus aroma and flavor. They are becoming more readily available, so ask for them where you buy Asian ingredients. If you can't find them fresh, they may be available frozen. Buy dried leaves as the last choice, and rehydrate them in boiling water for at least 10 minutes before use, allowing 4 to 5 dried leaves for every 3 fresh leaves called for in a recipe. Some recipes specify *fresh* leaves and these alternatives cannot be used in most cases. Fresh common lime zest or dried kaffir lime zest is another substitute. Allow 2 small strips of fresh zest or 3 small strips of dried zest for each leaf called for in a recipe, soaking dried zest in boiling water for 7 to 10 minutes before use. Crush or score fresh leaves to exploit their true brilliance.

KECAP MANIS: A thick, sweet variation of soy sauce, it gives deep color and a molasses flavor to sauces, and is used as a condiment and dipping sauce. The Indonesian *kecap manis* is more commonly available than the thick soy sauce used occasionally in Thailand. See also Soy Sauce.

LEMONGRASS: One of the signature herbs in Thai cooking. Fresh is by far the best, as dried lemongrass has a peppery taste that's quite different from the lemony-lime fragrance and intense citrus taste of the fresh. Use only the lower, tightly furled base section of this long-leaved herb. Chop it very, very finely (see notes on preparation, page 12) if using raw, and fine enough that it can be ground to a paste when preparing for curry pastes. When using whole, slit lengthwise or bruise with a rolling pin to release its full aroma. Strips of lime zest are an adequate substitute.

LIMES: Freshly squeezed limes are favored in the Thai kitchen, although lemon or bottled lime juice will suffice if necessary.

MUSHROOMS: Wild and cultivated mushrooms are found in abundance in Thailand. Thai cooks use several types. **Abalone mushrooms** are large and fleshy, and resemble *shiitake*. Sold canned, a 19-ounce can of abalone mushrooms yields 12 ounces drained mushrooms, about 1½ cups. Fresh or dried **black Chinese mushrooms** (Japanese shiitake) are intensely aromatic. Rehydrate dried by soaking, and use the water in the recipe if specified to do so. Keep dried mushrooms in an airtight container. **Golden mushrooms** are Japanese *enokitake*, sold fresh in clumps just as they are removed from the tree on which they grow, or in cans of 14 ounces, which yield about 1 cup (8 ounces) drained mushrooms. **Oyster mushrooms** are elegant, pearly gray, irregularly shaped mushrooms that are sold fresh. They have a subtle flavor that is shown to its best in soups and stir-fries. It is the small, ball-shaped **straw mushroom** that is most favored in Thai cooking. They are sold in cans of 14 ounces, which yield about 1 cup (7 ounces) drained mushrooms. If you are lucky, the label will specify "small," which is what you want for most of these recipes. Unused canned mushrooms should be decanted into a glass or plastic storage container, covered with cooled, boiled water, and refrigerated. Drained and recovered with fresh cooled, boiled water every day, they will keep for up to 1 week. If the fresh variety of any of these mushrooms is available, use them. Fresh button mushrooms are only a good substitute if very small, however. Canned button mushrooms will do in a pinch.

NOODLES: Many different noodles are used in Thai cooking. Most of the more popular noodles are made from rice flour. *Sen lek* are flat rice stick noodles used for making the classic noodle dish *pad thai*, while *sen yai* are broad rice noodles usually purchased fresh. *Sen mee* are the fine filaments of rice vermicelli that expand to a fluffy white cloud when fried, and to a snowy softness when cooked in water. Other noodles of importance in Thai cooking are *be mee*, egg noodles that may be made from wheat or rice flour, or a mixture of both. *Wun sen* are often mistaken for rice vermicelli, but are in fact made from a type of mung bean flour, which makes them semitranslucent and slippery when cooked. These noodles are variously called bean thread vermicelli, bean threads, glass noodles, or transparent vermicelli. They should be soaked in boiling water, and require little cooking, but can be simmered for ages in a slow-cooked dish without turning mushy. Lesser known are *kanom jin*, fine rice noodles that are used in many festive dishes.

ONIONS: See The Essentials, page 13.

OYSTER MUSHROOMS: See mushrooms.

OYSTER SAUCE: See vegetarian mushroom oyster sauce.

PALM SUGAR: While white or brown cane sugar is an adequate replacement for the palm sugar used in many Thai dishes, the real thing is sold in any good Asian store and is not expensive, so why not aim for authenticity? Like cane sugar, soft-textured, moist palm sugar undergoes various processes that render the finished product from light in color to a caramelized smoky dark brown. I have specified which to use in the recipes. For the lighter-colored palm sugar, which is sweet and mild in taste, use superfine white sugar as an alternative, unless otherwise specified. For the medium-light palm sugar, substitute raw sugar or a soft light brown sugar. You will need a richly flavored dark sugar to replace dark palm sugar.

RICE: In Thailand, long-grain white rice and "sticky," or glutinous, rice are both eaten. Jasmine, with its slender grains and heavenly aroma, is the favored rice in Thailand, although many different varieties are grown there. It is now marketed or grown in many countries, and has an elegance and distinct fragrance that make it the perfect accompaniment to Thai food. If you can't find it, or afford it, never mind. Any good long-grain white rice will do. Glutinous rice is, contrary to the implication of its name, low in gluten. It is a long-grain rice, available both black and white, that becomes quite starchy and gluelike when cooked, causing it to stick together densely. In northern Thailand, steamed "sticky" white rice is served in small baskets with the meal, to be eaten from the fingers like bread. Black rice is used for puddings.

RICE FLOUR: Flour made from finely milled regular rice, or from high-starch glutinous rice, has various applications in Thai cooking, particularly when making sweets. Check the label carefully when buying, as "sticky" (glutinous) rice flour cannot be substituted for common rice flour.

ROASTED CHILI POWDER AND PASTE: See The Essentials, page 13.

SALT-PICKLED MUSTARD GREENS: Mustard cabbage, a type of kale, is pickled in a salt brine. It has an intense saltiness, so should be rinsed before use. It is sold by weight, or in glazed ceramic jars, bottles, or cans. Substitute salt-pickled radish, Japanese radish pickles, dill cucumbers, or Korean *kimchi*, drained and rinsed to reduce their pungency.

SALT-PICKLED RADISHES: Japanese white radish, sliced and pickled in salted rice mash. Sold in Japanese stores. See salt-pickled mustard greens for substitutes.

SAMBAL ULEK: Whenever I need well-flavored crushed chili for a dish, I reach for my jar of Indonesian *sambal ulek*. It's simply red chilies ground with salt, but it's always an intense red, and is wonderously fragrant. Sichuan chili paste or your own favorite brand will do, or make it yourself by smashing red chilies in a mortar with salt. Keep it refrigerated.

SCALLIONS: No other ingredient presents cookbook writers with the dilemma that arises around explaining onions and their relatives. Scallions are variously known as green onions and spring onions, and sometimes even as shallots, depending on what you're reading or where you're shopping at the time. Firm, slim white bases and long, hollow green stems describe what we need for these recipes. See also The Essentials, page 13.

SHALLOTS: See The Essentials, page 13.

SHRIMP PASTE: See The Essentials, page 11.

SNAKE BEANS: See Chinese long beans.

SOY SAUCE: A sauce made of salt-fermented soybeans, of which three types are used. Light soy is an amber-brown, salty sauce used as a condiment, and in cooking when a light, salty taste is called for. It is also known as thin soy sauce. Dark soy sauce is thicker, less salty in taste, and deeper in color, so is used in cooking to create dark sauces of intense flavor. Thick soy sauce is the consistency of a syrup, and is used principally for coloring. See also *kecap manis*.

STRAW MUSHROOMS: See mushrooms.

SWEET POTATOES: Several varieties of sweet potatoes and yams grow in Thailand. Golden sweet potatoes have an orange-buff skin and bright, golden flesh, while red sweet potatoes have a gray-pink flesh and are slightly sweeter. They are interchangeable in these recipes, unless otherwise specified.

TAMARIND: A tart, fleshy seasoning product obtained from the pods of tamarind trees. It is valued for its tangy flavor, which heightens other tastes around it. For convenience, use concentrated tamarind straight from the jar, or buy whole tamarind pulp with seeds, and extract the flavored water by soaking and kneading in hot water. If unavailable, substitute lemon juice, using approximately twice the specified amount for tamarind concentrate and equal quantities for tamarind water.

TARO: This firm-textured root vegetable makes cameo appearances in Thai cooking, and is a particularly useful vegetarian ingredient, appreciated for its dense, "meaty" texture. Sweet potato, yam, or potato can replace it in most recipes.

TEMPEH: This mass of compressed, fermented soybeans, which was first made in Indonesia, has become a popular ingredient in vegetarian cooking. Like tofu, it's remarkably versatile, and is readily available where health foods are sold.

TOFU: The soybean is singularly one of the most important food plants in the world. From it comes a range of products that contribute significantly to the diet and health of vegetarians around the world. Protein-rich bean curd, now more commonly known by its Japanese name *tofu* (the term I use in this book), is *tao hoo* in Thailand. I have employed it extensively in my recipes, with no apology. Few other food products can match its versatility or its goodness. For most recipes, I've asked for a firm tofu, which means one that gives some resistance when pressed, unlike the soft, fresh product that crushes easily. Firm tofu can be shredded, chopped, or minced, as a recipe requires, and is positively wonderful when fried to golden brown to eat on its own, with a sauce, or to cook further in stir-fries, soups, braised dishes, or curries. Soft and firm tofu can be kept in the refrigerator in the container in which they were purchased for up to 3 days. Freezing tofu is not advisable, as its smooth texture is changed to something porous, chewy, and spongelike in the freezer.

Fried tofu comes in several forms: large blocks of about 7 inches long by 4 inches wide by 1 inch thick, smaller pieces about 2½ inches square by 1 inch thick, and cubes of about 1½ inches. Basically, fried tofu is firm, fresh bean curd that has been fried until the surface is golden brown, while the inside remains soft and dense. Different types of fried tofu undergo differing rates of frying to achieve specific effects. While continued frying does not change the outer surface much, the pieces become almost hollow as their insides cook away. The smaller cubes of fried tofu that are firm and elastic on the surface and almost hollow inside are best in braised and slow-simmered dishes, and are useful for stuffing. Before adding it to a dish, fried tofu should be rinsed well in boiling water or soaked for about 10 minutes in hot water to remove stale surface oils, then drained well or dried before use. Fried tofu can be stored in the refrigerator in a plastic bag for several weeks, and can be frozen.

Bean curd sheets or skins and sticks are formed when a hot solution of the soybean "milk" used to make bean curd is cooled and develops a skin on top. This skin is lifted off and dried in sheets or folded sticks, both of which add texture, body, and protein to vegetarian dishes. The sheets are used to wrap foods for steaming, frying, or poaching, and the sticks are cut into pieces to add directly to a dish as a main ingredient. To use dried bean curd sheets or sticks, soften them first in cold water, then partially dry them by spreading them on a towel before use, handling them with care. When deep-fried, the sticks or foods wrapped in the sheets acquire an appetizing light and crisp texture.

VEGETARIAN GLUTEN: See wheat gluten.

VEGETARIAN MUSHROOM OYSTER SAUCE: This vegetarian adaptation of the thick, salty Chinese oyster sauce is a glossy, smooth sauce with all the flavor appeal of its seafood-based role model. Ask for it where you buy Asian foods, or try your health-foods shop. See also The Essentials, page 11.

WATER SPINACH: This is one of the most popular vegetables in Thailand, where it grows prolifically along the *klongs* (waterways), earning it the name water vegetable, or *pak bung*. It has long, hollow stems, slender green leaves, and a flavor similar to spinach, which can substitute in any recipe.

WHEAT GLUTEN: Extracted from wheat, this spongy product is a useful meat substitute in vegetarian cooking. Sold by health-food suppliers, and also found in the freezer cabinet of well-stocked Asian food stores, it is used in braised dishes and stir-fries, in much the same way as fried tofu, which can be substituted.

WHITE FUNGUS: See black fungus.

WONTON SKINS: These 3½-inch squares or 3-inch rounds of silky-textured pasta resemble superfine lasagna pasta and are made in the same way, from a dough of wheat flour and eggs. They are sold fresh or frozen in blocks of about 40 pieces. The fresh wrappers can be kept wrapped in plastic in the refrigerator for about 5 days.

YELLOW BEAN SAUCE: A salty seasoning of whole yellow soybeans fermented in brine. In these recipes, it has been useful in producing alternatives to the seafood products used in curry pastes and sauces. See also The Essentials, page 11.

CHAPTER TWO

STARTERS

AND SNACKS

# STARTERS AND SNACKS

ACLUSTER OF UMBRELLA-COVERED FOOD STANDS IN A MARKETPLACE, A ROADSIDE TRUCK STOP, AN OPEN-FRONTED CAFE, AN ITINERANT FOOD HAWKER WITH PORTABLE CHARCOAL COOKER ON A STREET CORNER—ALL ARE PLACES WHERE SOME OF THE BEST FOOD IN THAILAND CAN BE BOUGHT. Many of the dishes presented as first courses at home or in a restaurant are snack foods that originated in such rustic kitchens. The range of small snacks in Thai cuisine is rich and varied, so the capricious purchase of a snack or sweetmeat at any time of the day is nowhere more natural than in Thailand.

Small dishes as first courses are rarely served one at a time in a dining-out situation. Instead, several different ones may be put out at once, for everyone to help themselves from the center of the table. At home, it is perfectly acceptable to offer a single first course, arranged on a platter or served on individual plates, so the number of servings included with the recipes is based on a single dish being served per course. As many Thai snack foods are perfect for party catering, however, each yield also indicates the number of individual pieces the recipe makes. In the latter case, plan to offer at least four pieces to each guest, depending on the occasion and the other foods being served.

# CARVED VEGETABLE PLATTER WITH SALTY EGG RELISH

MAKES ABOUT ¾ CUP; SERVES 4 TO 6 AS A FIRST COURSE, OR 10 OR MORE AS A DIP

THERE ARE MANY TYPES OF PUNGENTLY FLAVORED RELISHES IN THAI CUISINE FOR SERVING AS DIPS WITH CRISP-FRIED SEAFOOD OR TOFU, OR ELABORATELY CARVED SALAD VEGETABLES. THIS REASON-ABLY HOT DIP, KNOWN AS **NAM PRIK KAI KEEM**, IS TRADITIONALLY MADE WITH SALTED DUCK EGGS, BUT IS EQUALLY SUCCESSFUL MADE WITH LARGE, UNSALTED CHICKEN EGGS.

To make the relish, place the eggs in a small saucepan with cold water to cover. Bring to a boil and reduce the heat slightly. Boil gently for 8 minutes, then lift out with a slotted spoon and place in a bowl of cold water to cover. Let stand for 1 minute, drain, and again cover with cold water. Set aside to cool completely.

Meanwhile, place the garlic and dried chilies in a wok or small iron pan with-out oil. Place over medium-low heat and cook, turning frequently, until the garlic is browned and partially softened and the chilies are a deep red-brown and very aromatic, about 8 minutes. Transfer to a mortar, spice grinder, or small food processor and pound or grind to a paste.

Peel the cooled eggs and separate the yolks. Discard the whites (or save to chop finely and use to garnish another dish) and incorporate the yolks into the paste. Then slowly add the remaining relish ingredients, one by one, in order, pounding or grinding between each addition, until you have a reasonably smooth sauce the consistency of thick cream. When done, the relish should be salty with a hint of sour and sweet and of medium heat. Adjust the seasoning, as required. The relish can be stored in a covered glass container in the refrigerator for about 5 days.

Prepare the salad vegetables and arrange them attractively on a platter. Cover with plastic wrap and chill for at least 1 hour or for up to 4 hours before serving. Serve the relish in several small dishes, for dipping.

NOTE: Allow at least 1 piece of each type of vegetable per person if serving as a party dip, or about 2 pieces of each per person if serving as a first course.

For the Salty Egg Relish

3 eggs

4 large garlic cloves

1 to 3 dried red chilies, seeded

1 ounce firm tofu (bean curd)

2 teaspoons fermented tofu, mashed with its brine

1 teaspoon tamarind concentrate, or 2 teaspoons freshly squeezed lemon juice

2 teaspoons light palm sugar or superfine white sugar

1 teaspoon salt

1½ tablespoons freshly squeezed lime or lemon juice

⅓ to ¾ cup water

For the Salad Platter

Carrot sticks; cucumber sticks; cucumber "leaves" (page 25); Japanese white radish sticks; celery sticks; Japanese pear slices; white Thai eggplants; mushrooms; green and red bell pepper; cherry tomatoes

# SALAD ROLLS IN RICE PAPER

MAKES 8 ROLLS; SERVES 4

ONE IS NEVER ENOUGH OF THESE DELICIOUS AND HEALTHFUL SALAD ROLLS. THEY ARE WRAPPED IN THE SAME SEMITRANSPARENT RICE PAPERS USED IN VIETNAMESE CUISINE. THE DRY PAPERS RESEMBLE DISKS OF BUFF-COLORED PLASTIC, WHICH, WHEN SOFTENED IN COLD WATER, TURN WHITE AND BECOME SOFT AND PLIABLE.

One by one, dip the dried rice papers into a bowl of cold water, leaving immersed long enough to soften and turn white, about 40 seconds, then carefully lift out and spread on a damp cloth.

The tofu can be used uncooked or fried. To fry, heat the oil in a small pan over medium-high heat and fry the tofu, turning as needed, until golden, about 2 minutes. Remove with tongs to paper towels to drain briefly.

Prepare all the vegetables and herbs as directed and arrange in groups on a board with the tofu. Divide the ingredients evenly among the rice-paper rounds, placing them one on top of the other in the center of each round. Wrap carefully first turning in one edge, then the two sides, and finally carefully rolling into a cylinder, taking care not to tear the rice paper.

To make the sauce, in a small bowl stir together the hoisin sauce and chili paste until well mixed, adjusting the chili paste to taste. Divide among small sauce dishes, for dipping.

Serve the salad rolls on small plates, with the sauce bowls alongside.

VARIATION: Use your own choice of salad ingredients in the filling, all cut into matchstick pieces. Consider jicama, snow peas, Japanese pear, Japanese white radish, and green bell pepper.

8 large Vietnamese rice papers (banh trang)

½ cup peanut oil or vegetable oil

¾ cup matchstick-cut firm tofu (bean curd)

8 tender whole lettuce leaves, or 1½ cups shredded lettuce

1 cup (3 ounces) bean sprouts, blanched for 15 seconds and drained

½ cup (2½ ounces) matchstick-cut celery

½ cup (2¼ ounces) matchstick-cut unpeeled, seeded cucumber

½ cup (2½ ounces) matchstick-cut peeled carrot, blanched in boiling water for 1 minute and drained

4 scallions, white and some green, cut into 3-inch pieces, then shredded lengthwise

1 mild fresh red chili or ¼ red bell pepper, seeded and finely shredded

8 small fresh mint or basil sprigs

8 small coriander (cilantro) sprigs

For the Sauce

½ cup hoisin sauce

¼ to ¾ teaspoon sambal ulek or other chili paste or sauce

# GREEN CHILI DIP

DRY-ROASTING GIVES HOT GREEN CHILIES A PLEASANTLY MILD, NUTTY FLAVOR THAT MAKES THIS POPULAR DIP, KNOWN AS **NAM PRIK NUM,** SUITABLE FOR ALL AGES AND TASTE PREFERENCES. SERVE IT WITH CRISP FRUIT AND VEGETABLE STICKS (SEE THE CARVED VEGETABLE PLATTER WITH SALTY EGG RELISH, PAGE 39). IT ALSO COMPLEMENTS NON-ASIAN ACCOMPANIMENTS SUCH AS CRACKERS OR BREAD STICKS. IN THAILAND, COOKS PAINSTAKINGLY GRIND THIS DIP BY HAND IN A STONE MORTAR; A BLENDER OR FOOD PROCESSOR ELIMINATES THE TEDIUM.

*1 cup fresh green chilies, seeded and coarsely chopped*

*8 to 10 garlic cloves*

*1 small yellow onion, coarsely chopped*

*4 cherry tomatoes, or 1 medium-sized, well-ripened tomato, cut in half*

*1 tablespoon coarsely chopped scallion, white and some green*

*3 or 4 fresh coriander (cilantro) sprigs, coarsely chopped*

*¼ to ½ cup water*

*1 tablespoon fermented tofu, mashed with its brine*

*1 tablespoon superfine white sugar, or to taste*

*2 to 4 teaspoons fish sauce, or light soy sauce*

*Salt, to taste, if using soy sauce*

Combine the chilies, garlic, onion and tomatoes in a heavy skillet without oil, over medium heat. Dry-roast, stirring and turning the ingredients frequently so they cook evenly, until well browned, about 14 minutes. Transfer to a mortar, blender, or food processor and pound or grind to a coarsely textured paste. Add the scallion and coriander and pound or grind again until reduced to a thick paste that retains some of its texture. While continuing to pound, or with the motor running, add up to ½ cup water, a teaspoon at a time, to make a mixture of pouring consistency.

Add the fermented tofu and sugar, and adjust the seasoning to taste with fish sauce, or light soy sauce and salt to taste, and give the mixture a brief final grind or process. Use immediately, pouring it into small bowls, or transfer to a jar to store in the refrigerator for up to 10 days.

NOTE: If you find the appearance of this dip unappealing, stir in a little finely chopped coriander (cilantro) just before serving, adding perhaps 1 teaspoon minced fresh red chili at the same time to brighten both color and taste.

# MARINATED QUAIL EGG AND CUCUMBER SKEWERS

THESE ELEGANT SKEWERS, CALLED **KHAI NOK KRA TA**, ARE A DELIGHT TO SERVE WITH DRINKS BEFORE A MEAL. PIERCE THEM WITH LONG TOOTHPICKS, AND SERVE ON A PLATTER ATOP A BED OF FINELY SHREDDED LETTUCE OR CARROT. AS A FIRST COURSE, DIVIDE THE INGREDIENTS AMONG 6 SKEWERS, 1 PER SERVING, AND PRESENT THEM ON CHILLED PLATES WITH LETTUCE AND FRESH HERBS.

In a stainless steel or glass bowl, combine the vinegar, white sugar, salt, and water, stirring to dissolve the sugar. Put the cucumber and carrot slices into the marinade and set aside for 30 minutes.

If using fresh quail eggs, place in a small saucepan with cold water to cover. Bring to a boil, reduce the heat to medium and cook gently for about 5 minutes. Lift out with a slotted spoon and place in a bowl of cold water to cover. When cool, peel them carefully. If using fresh chicken eggs, cook in the same way, increasing the cooking time to 8 minutes, then cool and peel. If using canned quail eggs, drain well. Place the quail eggs in a bowl.

In a small saucepan over medium heat, warm the oil. Add the garlic and chili paste and fry, stirring continuously, until fragrant, about 1½ minutes. Add the ginger, soy sauce, and palm or brown sugar to taste, and cook, stirring, for 30 seconds. Pour the sauce over the eggs and allow them to marinate for 15 minutes, turning frequently.

To assemble, remove the cucumber and carrot slices from the marinade. If using toothpicks, pierce a single piece of cucumber and carrot with each toothpick, then add a whole quail egg. If preparing as a first course, thread the cucumber and carrot and the quail eggs onto the skewers, alternating them. If you are using chicken eggs, cut them in half crosswise and dip the cut surface into the marinade before threading them onto the skewers or toothpicks.

Arrange the toothpicks on a platter over shredded lettuce or carrot, or the skewers on plates garnished with small lettuce leaves and herbs, and serve.

NOTE: The skewers can be assembled up to 1 hour ahead, covered with plastic wrap, and refrigerated.

¼ cup distilled white vinegar

2½ tablespoons superfine white sugar

¾ teaspoon salt

⅓ cup water

3 small cucumbers, unpeeled, each 4 to 5 inches long (about 8 ounces total weight), cut into ½-inch-thick slices

18 very thin carrot slices

18 fresh quail eggs, 1 can (15 ounces) quail eggs in brine (contains approximately 18 eggs), or 9 small chicken eggs

1 tablespoon vegetable oil

½ to 1 teaspoon minced garlic

½ teaspoon sambal ulek or other chili paste

2 teaspoons minced or grated fresh ginger

⅓ cup dark soy sauce

1 to 2 tablespoons medium-light palm sugar or soft brown sugar

For Serving

Finely shredded lettuce or carrot

Small whole lettuce leaves and fresh herb sprigs, if using skewers

6 thin wooden skewers, each 8 inches long, or 18 long toothpicks

# "GALLOPING HORSES"

MAKES 24; SERVES 4 TO 6

**N**O ONE SEEMS TO KNOW WHY THESE POPULAR THAI HORS D'OEUVRES CAME TO BE NAMED **MA HOR**, WHICH TRANSLATES AS "GALLOPING HORSES." THE CLASSIC VERSION HAS SWEET-HOT PORK AND PEANUTS SERVED ON TROPICAL FRUIT, WHILE THIS MODERATELY HOT VEGETARIAN VERSION USES A TOPPING OF BEAN CURD AND SHIITAKE MUSHROOMS ON FRUITS SUCH AS HONEYDEW MELON, MANGO, JAPANESE PEAR, PAPAYA, ORANGE, TANGERINE, OR MANDARIN. THEY CAN BE SERVED AS A SHARED COURSE OR SIDE DISH, OR THE MIXTURE SEVED OVER LETTUCE AS A FIRST COURSE WITH GREEN PAPAYA SALAD (PAGE 80).

*24 pieces fresh fruit (see above), each 1½ inches square and ⅓ inch thick, or citrus segments, butterfly cut and opened*

*1 ounce dried bean curd skin, soaked in hot water to cover for 5 minutes*

*2 ounces fresh shiitake mushrooms, or ½ ounce dried black mushrooms*

*5 tablespoons peanut oil*

*6 ounces firm tofu (bean curd), diced*

*3 large garlic cloves, finely chopped*

*1 tablespoon minced yellow onion*

*1½ teaspoons Red Curry Paste (page 14)*

*1 tablespoon dark palm sugar or dark brown sugar*

*2 tablespoons chunky peanut butter*

*⅓ cup coconut cream*

*Salt and freshly ground black pepper, to taste*

*¼ cup (1 ounce) minced water chestnuts*

*½ teaspoon sambal ulek*

*1 to 2 teaspoons lime or lemon juice*

*Coriander or basil leaves, for garnish*

*Fine fresh red chili strips, for garnish*

Arrange the fruit on a platter, cover with plastic wrap, and refrigerate.

Drain the bean curd skin and pat dry with a kitchen towel. Roll it up and, using scissors or a sharp knife, cut into fine shreds, then chop it finely. If using dried mushrooms, soak in warm water to cover for 20 minutes, drain well, squeeze out any water, and trim stems. Chop the fresh or dried mushrooms finely.

In a wok or skillet over medium-high heat, heat the oil. Add the tofu, bean curd skin, and mushrooms and cook, stirring, until slightly crisped, about 6 minutes. Remove with a slotted spoon to a plate and pour off all but 1 tablespoon of the oil from the pan.

Add the garlic and shallots or onion to the same pan and cook over medium heat until lightly colored, about 4 minutes. Return the tofu mixture to the pan and add the curry paste. Stir well and cook for about 1½ minutes, until fragrant. Add the sugar, peanut butter, coconut cream, and salt and pepper and cook for 2 minutes, stirring continuously. Reduce the heat to medium-low, add the water chestnuts, and chili paste, and cook, stirring frequently, until the mixture is very thick, 8 to 10 minutes. Check the seasoning and then remove from the heat. Stir in the lime or lemon juice. Spoon into a bowl and set aside to cool.

To finish the dish, place a teaspoon of the tofu mixture on each piece of fruit. Garnish with coriander basil leaves and chili strips.

NOTE: This dish can be made up to 2 hours in advance, and refrigerated until ready to serve.

# "FISH" CAKES

MAKES 24; SERVES 4 TO 6

THE SUCCESS OF THESE VELVETY TEXTURED CAKES, THAT EMULATE THE POPULAR NONVEGETARIAN THAI FISH CAKES CALLED **TOD MUN PLA**, LIES IN THE VERY FINE SLICING OF THE SUPPLEMENTARY INGREDIENTS. THEY ARE BEST CAREFULLY SLICED WITH A SHARP KNIFE, RATHER THAN CHOPPED UNEVENLY IN A FOOD PROCESSOR. THE QUANTITIES ARE SMALL, SO IT IS NOT TOO ONEROUS A TASK.

*1 pound firm tofu (bean curd)*

*1 teaspoon Red Curry Paste (page 14).*

*1 tablespoon light soy sauce*

*2 teaspoons fermented tofu*

*1 tablespoon all-purpose flour*

*1 egg (optional)*

*4 teaspoons Crisp-Fried Garlic (page 24)*

*4 kaffir lime leaves, very, very finely
    shredded, or 1 teaspoon grated lime zest*

*½ cup (2 ounces) very, very finely
    sliced long beans, green beans or
    slender asparagus spears*

*¼ cup (1 ounce) very, very finely
    chopped water chestnuts*

*¼ cup (1 ounce) very, very finely
    chopped scallions*

*1 tablespoon very, very finely chopped
    fresh coriander (cilantro)*

*1 small, hot fresh green chili, seeded and
    minced*

*3 to 4 cups corn or other vegetable oil*

*Cucumber Vinegar Sauce (page 21)
    or Sweet Chili Sauce (page 18)*

To make the cakes, place the firm tofu in a food processor. Add the curry paste, soy sauce, fermented tofu, rice flour or all-purpose flour and the egg, if using. Process until thoroughly mixed. Add the Crisp-Fried Garlic, lime leaves, beans, water chestnuts, scallions, coriander, and chili, and pulse just long enough to mix. Do not pulverize. Alternatively, mix together in a large bowl, working until the ingredients are thoroughly amalgamated.

To cook the cakes, pour the oil into a wok or a large, deep pan, and heat to 375 degrees F. Plan on cooking in two or three batches, so the oil maintains its heat. Using 2 wet tablespoons, shape the tofu mixture into ovals the size of the spoon, slide each into the hot oil as it is made, until you have about 8 cakes frying. Reduce the heat slightly, and cook them until golden brown, turning once or twice, about 1½ minutes. Retrieve with a slotted spoon and drain briefly on paper towels. Cook and drain the remaining batches of cakes in the same way.

Arrange the cakes on a platter or on individual plates and serve with one of the suggested sauces, as a dip or poured over the top.

# GRILLED VEGETABLES WITH CHILI RELISH

SERVES 4 TO 6

**Y**OU ARE UNLIKELY TO FIND GRILLED VEGETABLES LIKE THESE ON A MENU IN THAILAND, BUT THEY ARE A GREAT SHOWCASE FOR THE SMOKY-CHILI INTENSITY OF MY CHILI RELISH.

Prepare a fire in a charcoal grill. Wipe the vegetables with a clean, damp cloth. Trim off the ends of the zucchini and eggplants, and cut them lengthwise into ⅛-inch-thick slices. Sprinkle lightly with salt. Cut the bell peppers or chilies in half and remove the stems and seeds. Cut the leeks into 2-inch lengths, including the tender greens. In a small cup, stir together the oils and brush the vegetables with them.

Put the vegetables on the grill rack about 4 inches above the fire, and grill, turning once or twice, until they are well flecked with brown and cooked crisp-tender. The grilling time will vary with the vegetables, but all of them should be ready in 5 to 7 minutes.

Arrange the grilled vegetables on warmed plates and sprinkle them with the lime leaf or coriander, if using. Serve with the Chili Relish on the plate or in individual dishes alongside.

NOTE: The vegetables can also be cooked in a cast-iron skillet or on a stove-top grill over medium-high heat.

*2 golden zucchini*

*2 green zucchini*

*2 or 3 slender Asian eggplants*

*Salt*

*4 to 6 small green bell peppers or mild fresh red chilies*

*4 to 6 young leeks*

*4 to 6 pieces pumpkin, each 2 inches square and ½ inch thick*

*2 tablespoons peanut or vegetable oil*

*2 teaspoons sesame oil*

*Very finely shredded fresh kaffir lime leaf or chopped fresh coriander (cilantro) leaves (optional)*

*Chili Relish (page 19)*

# EGGS IN SWEET AND SPICY SAUCE

SERVES 4 TO 6

THIS DISH OF HARD-COOKED EGGS IN A SPICY SAUCE WITH NUANCES OF HOT CHILI AND THE SWEET-NESS OF PALM SUGAR AND PINEAPPLE IS CALLED **KAI LOOK KOEY** IN THAILAND. IT IS A PALATE-PLEASING START TO A MEAL, BUT CAN ALSO ACCOMPANY CURRIES.

6 chicken or duck eggs

1 teaspoon distilled white vinegar

2 cups peanut or vegetable oil

½ cup (ounces) finely sliced shallots or
    yellow onions

½ cup rice flour

½ cup all-purpose flour

½ cup coconut cream or coconut milk

1 tablespoon dark palm sugar or dark
    brown sugar

1½ tablespoons thick sweet soy sauce
    (kecap manis)

3 tablespoons pineapple juice or syrup
    from canned pineapple

1½ teaspoons sambal ulek, chili bean
    paste, or other chili sauce

1 large garlic clove, crushed

Salt, to taste

Small lettuce leaves, for garnish

1½ tablespoons Crisp-Fried Shallots
    (page 24), or 2 tablespoons sliced
    scallion greens, for garnish

1 large, mild fresh red chili, seeded and
    finely shredded, for garnish

Place the eggs in a saucepan with cold water to cover and add the vinegar. Bring to a boil, reduce the heat slightly, and boil gently for 8 minutes. Lift out with a slotted spoon and place in a bowl of cold water to cover. Let stand for 1 minute, drain, and again cover with cold water. Let cool completely, peel, and set aside.

Pour the oil into a wok or large, deep pan and heat to medium-hot. Add the sliced shallots or onions and fry until they are well browned, about 4 minutes. Retrieve with a slotted spoon and drain on paper towels.

In a bowl, combine the rice flour and all-purpose flour and stir in the coconut cream or coconut milk and enough cold water to form a batter of coating consistency. Cut the eggs in half lengthwise and dip them into the batter, coating evenly. Reheat the oil. Carefully slip the eggs into the oil, no more than 6 halves at a time, and fry, turning several times, until golden brown, about 1½ minutes. Retrieve with a slotted spoon and set aside to drain. Cook and drain the remaining eggs in the same way, then pour off all but about 1½ tablespoons of oil from the pan.

To make the sauce, heat the 1½ tablespoons oil over medium heat. Add the sugar, sweet soy sauce, pineapple juice or syrup, *sambal ulek* or other chili sauce, and garlic. Stir well and simmer until the sauce has reduced slightly, about 5 minutes. Season to taste with salt. Place the eggs into the pan and turn them over a few times in the sauce, until coated evenly.

To serve, arrange the lettuce leaves on individual plates, and place the eggs on top. Garnish with the fried shallots or scallion greens, and the chili shreds, and serve at once.

NOTE: The eggs can be allowed to cool in the sauce, and served cold.

# GOLDEN SPRING ROLLS

MAKES 24: SERVES 4 TO 6

**D**OH PIA TAWT, AS THEY ARE CALLED IN THAILAND, ARE CRISP PASTRY ROLLS FILLED WITH A RAINBOW OF SHREDDED VEGETABLES. THEY ARE SERVED WITH THE TART CUCUMBER VINEGAR SAUCE ON PAGE 21, OR THE TANGY SWEET CHILI SAUCE ON PAGE 18. SPRING ROLL WRAPPERS ARE SOLD AT ASIAN STORES. DRIED BEAN CURD SKINS, SOAKED FIRST TO SOFTEN THEM, ARE AN ALTERNATIVE WRAPPER; SEE PAGE 34.

*24 small fresh or frozen spring roll skins (wrappers), or enough dried bean curd skin to make twenty-four 6-inch squares*

*½ ounce bean thread vermicelli*

*3 ounces firm tofu (bean curd), cut into short, fine strips*

*2 scallions, including some green, cut into 1½-inch pieces, shredded*

*¼ cup (1¼ ounces) finely shredded bamboo shoots*

*¼ cup (1 ounce) finely shredded carrot, blanched and drained*

*¼ cup (1¾ ounces) sliced straw mushrooms or abalone mushrooms*

*¼ cup (1½ ounces) unsalted roasted peanuts, chopped*

*1 large, mild fresh red chili, shredded*

*1 tablespoon light soy sauce*

*½ teaspoon salt*

*¼ teaspoon white pepper*

*2 tablespoons chopped fresh coriander*

*1 tablespoon finely shredded ginger*

*3 to 4 cups peanut or corn oil*

*Cucumber Vinegar Sauce (page 21) or Sweet Chili Sauce (page 18)*

If the spring roll skins are frozen, place them in a warm part of the kitchen, cover with a cloth, and leave for about 25 minutes, to soften. When pliable, separate them but keep them covered to prevent them from drying out. If using the bean curd skin for wrappers, moisten them in warm water until softened, 2 to 5 minutes, then drain well. Carefully cut into 6-inch squares, and spread on a lightly dampened kitchen towel. Cover with another dampened towel until needed.

To make the filling, soak the vermicelli for 10 minutes, drain well, and use kitchen shears or a sharp knife to cut into 1-inch lengths. Place in a mixing bowl and add the tofu, scallions, bamboo shoots, carrot, mushrooms, peanuts, chili, soy sauce, salt, pepper, coriander, and ginger, mixing them together thoroughly but carefully.

Working with 1 wrapper at a time, place a portion of the filling in the center of a wrapper, fold over one end on the diagonal to form a triangle, then fold in the sides, and roll up. Moisten the end with water and gently squeeze the roll to seal the end. As you form the spring rolls, place them on a tray, taking care they do not stick together.

To fry the spring rolls, pour the oil into a wok or a large, deep pan and heat to about 395 degrees F. Plan to cook the spring rolls in three batches so the oil maintains its heat. Carefully slide one-third of the spring rolls into the oil and fry, turning them several times, until golden brown, about 2 minutes. Retrieve with a slotted spoon and drain on a rack covered with paper towels. Cook and drain the remaining two batches in the same way. Serve as soon as possible after frying, with Cucumber Vinegar Sauce or Sweet Chili Sauce.

# MUSHROOMS, PEANUTS, AND TOFU IN LETTUCE ROLLS

MAKES 12; SERVES 6

A MILDLY SPICED FILLING OF TOFU, MUSHROOMS, AND PEANUTS IS WRAPPED IN CRUNCHY LETTUCE LEAVES TO EAT LIKE A SANDWICH — HANDS-ON ENJOYMENT AT AN INFORMAL MEAL.

Drain the mushrooms, strain and reserve the soaking water, and squeeze out excess water. Trim off the mushroom stems, cutting close to the caps, then finely chop the mushrooms and set aside. Drain the black fungus, trim off any woody parts, and chop them finely.

Pour the oil into a wok or large, deep pan and heat to 395 degrees F. Slip the dry rice vermicelli into the oil and fry for about 45 seconds. It will quickly expand to a white mass, and then turn a light gold. Flip and cook the other side until lightly golden, about 30 seconds. Retrieve with a slotted spoon or wire skimmer and drain on a rack covered with paper towels. Leave to cool.

Reduce the heat slightly, and add the shallots or onion. Fry, stirring them constantly so they cook evenly, until they are well browned, about 4 minutes. Remove with a slotted spoon to paper towels to drain. Pour off all but 1½ table-spoons of the oil, reserving it for use in another recipe.

Reheat the wok or pan over high heat and add the scallions, garlic, ginger, lemongrass, and chili. Stir-fry until fragrant, about 1½ minutes. Add the mush-rooms, black fungus, tofu, and peanuts, and stir over high heat for 30 seconds, then reduce the heat to medium. Season with the soy and hoisin sauces and the sugar and cook, stirring frequently, for 3 to 4 minutes longer to blend the flavors.

Combine the cornstarch with ⅔ cup of the reserved mushroom water and pour into the pan. Cook, stirring slowly, until the mixture thickens, 1 to 2 min-utes. Crumble in the fried rice vermicelli and the fried shallots or onion, stir well, and cook for a minute or so over medium heat. Season with salt and pepper and add the lime or lemon juice and coriander. Transfer to a serving dish.

To serve, place a generous spoonful of the filling in a lettuce cup, and add a dab of the sauce, fold in the sides of the lettuce, and roll up. Dip into the sauce again and enjoy.

6 dried black mushrooms, soaked in 1
    cup boiling water for 15 minutes
¼ cup (¼ ounce) shredded dried black
    (wood ear) fungus, soaked in hot
    water for 15 minutes
1½ cups peanut or vegetable oil
¼ pound rice vermicelli (sen mee)
1 small yellow onion, chopped
2 scallions, white and green, finely sliced
2 garlic cloves, minced
1½ teaspoons minced fresh ginger
2 teaspoons minced lemongrass
½ to 2 teaspoons minced fresh red chili
10 ounces firm tofu (bean curd), diced
½ cup (2½ ounces) unsalted roasted
    peanuts, chopped
1 tablespoon light soy sauce
1 tablespoon hoisin sauce
1 teaspoon dark palm or brown sugar
1 tablespoon cornstarch
Salt and freshly ground black pepper, to taste
Freshly squeezed lime or lemon juice, to taste
1 tablespoon chopped fresh coriander
12 well-chilled cup-shaped lettuce leaves
½ to ¾ cup hoisin sauce, Sweet Chili
    Sauce (page 18), or Cucumber
    Vinegar Sauce (page 21)

# LITTLE MUSHROOM SOUFFLÉS FLAVORED WITH RED CURRY PASTE AND BASIL

SERVES 6 TO 8

IN THAILAND, LITTLE CHILI-SPICED SOUFFLÉS OF PUREED SEAFOOD OR VEGETABLES, KNOWN AS **MUK HET**, ARE STEAMED IN SMALL CONTAINERS MADE FROM STRIPS OF FOLDED BANANA LEAF. THEY CAN BE COOKED IN SMALL RAMEKINS OR CHINESE TEACUPS TO SERVE AS A FIRST COURSE, AN INTERESTING INTERMEZZO BETWEEN COURSES, OR AS ONE OF SEVERAL MAIN COURSES SERVED SIMULTANEOUSLY, IN THE THAI TRADITION. WHILE THE EGGS MAKE THE SOUFFLÉS LIGHTER IN TEXTURE AND HELP TO BIND THE INGREDIENTS, THEY CAN BE OMITTED.

Combine the rice and coconut cream in a small saucepan and place over medium-high heat. Bring to a boil, reduce heat slightly, and cook for about 6 minutes until the mixture is quite thick. At the same time, boil the peas in lightly salted water until almost tender, about 4 minutes for frozen, 12 minutes for fresh. Drain well.

Place the oyster mushrooms in a food processor or blender and chop finely. Remove one-third of the mushrooms and transfer to a bowl. Add 2 tablespoons of the rice mixture and the sugar and salt to the food processor or blender and process until reasonably smooth. Add the processed mixture to the bowl holding the chopped mushrooms along with the remaining rice mixture, the cooked peas, curry paste, and eggs. Beat until smooth.

Brush the inside of 6 to 8 small ramekins with the oil and place a basil leaf in each. Spoon in the mixture and smooth the tops. Place the whole kaffir lime leaves or basil leaves in the water container of a steamer, with hot water to a depth of 2 inches. Place the ramekins on the steamer rack, cover, and bring the water to a boil. Reduce the heat slightly and steam the soufflés until they are firm to the touch, about 25 minutes. Remove from the steamer and let cool completely, then turn the soufflés out onto individual plates.

While the soufflés are cooling, prepare the garnish. Pour the coconut cream into a small saucepan and bring to a boil, reduce heat to low, and simmer gently until reduced by almost half, about 12 minutes. Let cool. To serve, spoon some of the reduced coconut cream over each soufflé, and decorate with chili strips and a few shreds of basil or kaffir lime leaves.

1 cup cooked white rice

1 cup coconut cream

½ cup (2 ounces) green peas (fresh or frozen)

8 ounces fresh oyster mushrooms, or 1 can (19 ounces) abalone mushrooms, drained

½ teaspoon superfine white sugar

½ teaspoon salt

½ to 1½ tablespoons Red Curry Paste (page 14)

2 eggs, beaten

2 teaspoons vegetable oil

6 to 8 large fresh basil leaves

3 kaffir lime leaves, or 8 to 10 large basil leaves (optional)

For the Garnish

¾ cup coconut cream

1 large, hot, fresh red chili, seeded and finely shredded

Very finely shredded fresh basil or kaffir lime leaves

# VEGETABLE DUMPLINGS

MAKES 24; SERVES 6

As a first course, serve these vegetable dumplings, known as **KHANOM KUI CHAI** in Thailand, on small warmed plates with a traditional Thai garnish of finely shredded carrot and sliced cucumber, and light soy or hot chili sauce for dipping. They are also convenient party food as they can be fried in advance and rewarmed in a heavy pan without oil to serve.

24 fresh or frozen wonton skins (wrappers), or enough dry bean curd skin to make twenty-four 6-inch squares

1 cup (5 ounces) peeled and cubed taro, sweet potato, or potato

½ cup (2½ ounces) finely chopped bamboo shoots

½ cup (3½ ounces) finely chopped straw mushrooms

¼ cup (1 ounce) cooked green peas or finely sliced green beans

½ cup (2½ ounces) unsalted roasted peanuts, chopped

½ cup (1½ ounces) minced scallions, white and some green, or garlic chives

2 large garlic cloves, minced

1 tablespoon minced or grated fresh ginger

1½ tablespoons chopped fresh coriander (cilantro)

2 tablespoons light soy sauce

½ teaspoon salt

¼ teaspoon white pepper

1 teaspoon sugar

1 cup peanut or vegetable oil (optional)

If the wonton wrappers are frozen, place them in a warm part of the kitchen, cover with a cloth, and leave for 30 minutes to soften. Moisten bean curd skin in warm water until softened, 2 to 5 minutes, then drain well. Carefully cut into 6-inch squares and spread on a lightly dampened kitchen towel. Cover with another dampened towel until needed.

Steam the taro, sweet potato, or potato over boiling water until tender, about 12 minutes. Alternatively, boil until tender. Transfer to a bowl and mash until smooth. Add the bamboo shoots, mushrooms, peas, peanuts, scallions, garlic, ginger, coriander, soy sauce, salt, pepper, and sugar, stirring and kneading until well mixed.

Work with 1 wonton wrapper at a time, to avoid their drying out. If using wonton skins, place 2 teaspoons of the mixture in the center of a wrapper. Moisten the edges of the wrapper with water and fold in the corners to overlap slightly, forming a small square parcel. Turn over so the ends are tucked underneath. If using squares cut from bean curd skin, place 2 tablespoons filling in the center of a square, fold the edge closest to you over the filling, fold in the two sides, and then finally fold over the last edge, moistening it with a little water.

Pour the oil into a large skillet or cast-iron pan over medium-high heat. When the oil is hot, slip about 12 dumplings into the oil. Fry, turning several times, until the surface of each is crisp and golden, about 2½ minutes. Carefully remove with tongs and set aside to drain on paper towels. When all of the dumplings have been fried, pour off the oil but do not wipe out the pan.

Reheat the pan over medium-high heat and return the dumplings to the pan, top facing downward. Cook for about 40 seconds, until golden and crisped. Turn and cook on the underside for about 40 seconds longer. Remove from the heat, and serve at once.

# FRIED TOFU WITH THREE SAUCES

SERVES 4

**B**ITE-SIZED CUBES OF FRIED TOFU ARE AN APPEALING FIRST COURSE WITH A MENU OF OTHER THAI DISHES OR A LARGE BOWL OF NOODLES. SERVE THEM ON A LETTUCE OR CABBAGE LEAF WITH A GARNISH OF SHREDDED CARROT AND CUCUMBER SLICES, AND ONE OR MORE OF THE SUGGESTED SAUCES. FRIED TOFU ALSO MAKES A QUICK AND TASTY SNACK THAT'S ENOUGH FOR A WHOLE MEAL IF YOU SERVE THE CUBES OVER WHITE RICE OR STIR-FRIED CHINESE CABBAGE. PURCHASE FRESH TOFU THAT IS FIRM ENOUGH TO CUT AND HANDLE WITHOUT CRUMBLING.

Cut the tofu into pieces of 1¼ by 1 by ½ inch. Prepare one or more of the sauces, and the ingredients for serving.

Pour the oil into a wok or a medium-sized skillet with high sides and heat to 375 degrees F. Add the tofu cubes and fry, turning frequently, until evenly golden brown, about 4½ minutes. Retrieve with a slotted spoon and drain briefly on paper towels.

As described in the introduction, arrange the tofu and its accompaniments on a serving plate, or divide among individual plates. If using a single sauce, pour it over the top, or serve it in small dishes for dipping. If using more than one, allow each diner to choose their own for dipping or spooning over the top.

VARIATION: Sticks of taro can be cooked in the same way as the tofu (they will require about 8 minutes of cooking) and served with the same dips, as a snack or simple first course.

*1 to 1¼ pounds firm tofu (bean curd)*
*2 cups peanut or vegetable oil, for deep frying*
*Sweet Chili Sauce (page 18)*
*Peanut Sauce (page 20)*
*Cucumber Vinegar Sauce (page 21)*

*Lettuce or cabbage leaves*
*Finely shredded carrot*
*Sliced cucumber*

# WONTONS WITH SESAME SOY SAUCE

MAKES 48; SERVES 4 TO 6

**K**HANOM IS THE THAI WORD FOR ANY BITE-SIZED SNACK, CAKE, OR SWEET, WHICH IN THIS INSTANCE INCLUDES THESE VELVETY-TEXTURED, VEGETABLE-FILLED WONTONS, WHICH ARE CALLED **KHANOM JIP.** THEY CAN, IF YOU PREFER, BE EATEN WITH THEIR POACHING BROTH AS A SOUP.

For the Wontons

48 fresh or frozen wonton skins (wrappers)

⅓ ounce dried black (wood ear) fungus,
   soaked in hot water for 15 minutes

1 small yellow onion, very finely chopped

¾ cup (3 ounces) finely diced cooked
   pumpkin or sweet potato

½ cup (2 ounces) cooked green peas

¼ cup (1½ ounces) chopped bamboo shoots

¼ cup (1¾ ounces) chopped straw,
   oyster, small button mushrooms

5 teaspoons minced fresh coriander
   (cilantro) root and leaves

2 teaspoons minced garlic

1 teaspoon minced or grated fresh ginger

1½ tablespoons vegetarian mushroom
   oyster sauce

1 tablespoon light soy sauce

2 tablepoons rice flour or all-purpose flour

First, make the wontons. If the wonton wrappers are frozen, place them in a warm part of the kitchen, cover with a cloth, and leave for 30 minutes to soften.

Drain the black fungus and trim off any woody bits. Chop it very finely and place in a bowl. Add all the remaining wonton ingredients except for 1 tablespoon of the flour. Mix thoroughly.

Working with 1 wonton wrapper at a time, place a heaped teaspoonful of the filling in the center of the wrapper. Moisten the edges of the wrapper with water and fold over to form a triangle, enclosing the filling. Press the edges to seal. As each wonton is formed, set it aside on a tray dusted with the remaining 1 tablespoon flour.

To make the sauce, in a small bowl, mix together the soy sauce, sesame oil, chili oil or minced chili, and sugar, stirring to dissolve the sugar. Stir in the coriander or scallion greens and divide among small bowls for dipping.

To cook the wontons, pour the water or stock into a large saucepan and add the oil, lime leaves or lemongrass, and ginger. Bring to a boil over high heat. Add one-third of the wontons and poach until cooked through and tender, about 2 minutes. Retrieve with a slotted spoon and place in a bowl, cover and set aside. Cook the remaining wontons in two batches, then return all the wontons to the liquid to reheat briefly.

Using the slotted spoon, transfer the wontons to individual bowls or shallow dishes, dividing them evenly. If serving as a soup, distribute the cooking liquid evenly among the bowls. Accompany with the dipping sauce.

VARIATION: The wontons can also be deep-fried. Omit the broth. In a wok or large, deep pan over medium-high heat, heat about 4 cups oil to 375 degrees F. Add 12 wontons and fry until golden brown, about 2 minutes. Retrieve with a slotted spoon and drain briefly on paper towels. Repeat with the remaining wontons in batches. Serve with hoisin sauce or a hot chili sauce for dipping.

For the Sauce

⅔ cup light soy sauce

2 tablespoons sesame oil

½ teaspoon chili oil, or 1 teaspoon minced hot fresh red chili

1 tablespoon superfine white sugar, or to taste

1 tablespoon minced fresh coriander (cilantro) or scallion greens

For the Broth

5 to 6 cups water or White Vegetable Stock (page 22)

1 to 2 teaspoons peanut, sesame or vegetable oil

2 kaffir lime leaves, or 1 lemongrass stalk, lightly bruised

4 thick slices fresh ginger

# SPICED CORN CAKES

MAKES 24 TO 30; SERVES 6 TO 8

RED CURRY PASTE GIVES A BITE TO THESE LIGHT AND CRUNCHY CORN CAKES, CALLED **TOD MAN KHAO POHD** IN THAILAND. IF YOU LIKE, REDUCE THE QUANTITY OF CORN AND REPLACE IT WITH FINELY DICED FIRM OR FRIED TOFU (BEAN CURD), VERY FINELY SLICED GREEN BEANS, OR PARBOILED FROZEN GREEN PEAS.

For the Cakes

3½ cups (14 ounces) corn kernels

1 cup (4 ounces) finely chopped celery
   with some leaves

½ cup all-purpose flour

2 tablespoons rice flour

2 teaspoons baking powder

1 to 1½ tablespoons Red Curry Paste
   (page 14)

1 tablespoon fish sauce or light soy sauce

½ teaspoon salt

1 egg white, lightly beaten (optional)

2 to 4 tablespoons water

2 tablespoons chopped fresh coriander
   (cilantro), optional

2 to 3 cups vegetable oil


Lettuce leaves (optional)

Cucumber Vinegar Sauce (page 21)

In a bowl, combine all of the ingredients for the corn cakes, except the oil, stirring to mix well. Set the mixture aside for about 10 minutes to allow time for the baking powder to activate.

Heat the oil in a large skillet or flat-bottomed wok over medium-high heat. Scoop up large teaspoonfuls of the corn mixture and drop carefully into the shallow oil. Fry, turning carefully once or twice with tongs or a slotted spoon, until golden and cooked through, about 3 minutes. Do not crowd the pan by cooking more than 8 to 10 at a time. Retrieve with a slotted spoon and drain on paper towels.

When all of the corn cakes are cooked and have drained for a few minutes, arrange them on a platter atop lettuce leaves or paper napkins. Serve the sauce in individual bowls, for dipping.

# MEE KROB OF CRISP RICE VERMICELLI WITH SWEET·SOUR FLAVORS

SERVES 4 TO 8

SWEET, CRISP **MEE KROB** MAKES AN INTERESTING FIRST COURSE, PERHAPS ACCOMPANIED WITH A SECOND DISH SUCH AS THE FRIED TOFU SERVED WITH SPICY PEANUT SAUCE (PAGE 55). OTHERWISE, SERVE THIS DISH AS IT IS SERVED IN THAILAND, TO ACCOMPANY CURRIES.

6 ounces rice vermicelli (sen mee)

5 ounces firm tofu (bean curd)

3 cups peanut or vegetable oil

For the Garnish

1 egg, lightly beaten with 1 tablespoon
    water (optional)

2 teaspoons peanut or vegetable oil, if needed

¾ cup (2¼ ounces) bean sprouts,
    blanched and refreshed

4 to 6 garlic chives or 2 scallions, white
    and green parts, cut into 1-inch pieces

1 large, mild fresh red or green chili,
    seeded and finely shredded

To Complete the Dish

3 or 4 garlic cloves, finely chopped

3 shallots, finely chopped

2½ tablespoons fish sauce or light soy sauce

2½ tablespoons distilled white vinegar

3 tablespoons dark palm sugar or dark
    brown sugar

½ teaspoon salt

½ teaspoon Roasted Chili Powder (page
13), plus extra for serving

Break up the bundle of noodles into two or three batches. Cut the tofu into thin strips, or into ½-inch cubes. Pour the oil into a wok or large, deep pan and heat to 395 degrees F. Slip a bundle of the noodles into the oil and fry for about 45 seconds. When it expands and turns a light gold, flip and cook the other side for about 15 seconds, then turn and refry the first side again for about 10 seconds, until lightly golden. Retrieve from the oil. Drain on a rack or plate lined with paper towels. Repeat with the remaining noodles.

Add the tofu and fry at the same heat, until golden brown and well crisped on the surface, about 2 minutes. Remove and drain on paper towels.

Next, prepare the garnish. If using the egg, heat a nonstick pan without oil, or a skillet with the 2 teaspoons of oil over medium heat. Pour in the beaten egg and tilt the pan and swirl the egg so it sets in a thin layer. When it is firm, flip and cook on the other side. Remove and set aside to cool.

Reheat 2 tablespoons of oil in wok or pan. Place over medium-high heat, add the garlic and shallots, and fry until golden brown, 1 to 1½ minutes. Remove with a slotted spoon and set aside. Add the fish sauce or soy sauce, the vinegar, sugar, and salt. Cook over medium-high heat, stirring often, until the mixture begins to caramelize, about 1 minute.

Add the Roasted Chili Powder and the cooked garlic, shallots and tofu. Cook, stirring, for 1 minute. Crumble the fried noodles into the pan and increase the heat to high. Using a wok spatula, stir and toss the ingredients together until the noodles are glazed with the sauce.

Turn onto a serving dish and surround with the garnishes. Roll up the egg crêpe and cut fine shreds. Drape over the noodles and serve at once, with extra Roasted Chili Powder.

# STEAMED RICE NOODLE ROLLS

MAKES 10 TO 12 ROLLS; SERVES 6

**T**HESE ROLLS MAKE A SUPERB LOW-CALORIE MEAL THAT CAN BE ENJOYED ALL THROUGH THE DAY, JUST AS THEY ARE IN THAILAND. YOU WILL NEED RICE NOODLE SHEETS, WHICH CAN BE PURCHASED IN ASIAN STORES.

If the rice noodle sheets are frozen, place them in a warm part of the kitchen for 20 minutes to soften. One at a time, dip fresh or thawed rice sheets into hot water to rinse off surface oil, then carefully spread on a kitchen towel to drain. They should be quite soft and pliable; if not, cover with plastic wrap and heat in a microwave for 30 seconds, or steam for a minute or so over boiling water. Set aside.

Drain the black fungus, squeeze out excess water, and chop finely, discarding any woody parts. Blanch the bean sprouts for 15 seconds in boiling water, drain, and refresh in ice water, then set aside in a colander to drain.

In a mortar or spice grinder, pound or grind the coriander roots, garlic cloves and the peppercorns. In a wok or skillet over medium-high heat, warm 2 tablespoons of the oil. Add the seasoning paste and fry, stirring frequently, until it is very aromatic, about 1½ minutes. Increase the heat to high, add the fungus and mushrooms, and stir-fry for 1 minute. Add the sugar, soy sauce, and hoisin sauce or bean paste. Cook for 1 minute, stirring continuously, then add the bean sprouts and scallions, mix well, and remove from the heat.

Spread some of the mixture evenly over the center of each rice sheet, leaving a 2-inch border on two sides, and roll up. Brush a heatproof plate or shallow dish with some of the remaining oil and arrange the noodle rolls on it side by side. Brush any oil that is left over the rolls. Set in a steamer over simmering water, cover the steamer, and steam until thoroughly heated through, about 15 minutes.

To serve, in a small bowl, combine the dark soy sauce, the oils and the sugar, stirring until the sugar has dissolved. When the rolls are ready, spoon the sauce evenly over them and scatter the scallion greens over them. Turn off the heat and let stand in the steamer, covered, for 2 minutes. Serve on the same plate.

## For the Rolls

1 pack (1¼ pounds) fresh or frozen rice noodle sheets

¼ ounce dried black (wood ear) fungus, soaked in hot water for 15 minutes

1½ cups (4½ to 5 ounces) bean sprouts

2 large fresh coriander (cilantro) roots

2 large garlic cloves

½ to 1 teaspoon black peppercorns

4 tablespoons vegetable oil

½ cup (3½ ounces) finely chopped oyster, straw, or abalone mushrooms

1 tablespoon medium-light palm sugar or soft brown sugar

1 tablespoon light soy sauce

1 tablespoon hoisin sauce, or 2 teaspoons chili bean paste

½ cup sliced scallions, white and green parts

## For Serving

2 tablespoons dark soy sauce

2 tablespoons peanut or vegetable oil

½ teaspoon sesame oil

1 teaspoon medium palm or brown sugar

¼ cup finely sliced scallion greens

CHAPTER THREE

❖

SOUPS AND

SALADS

# SOUPS

IN MOST ASIAN CUISINES, A MEAL IS NOT COMPLETE WITHOUT A SOUP, AND THAILAND IS NO EXCEPTION. For many, the day begins with a bowl of *khao tom*, a rice gruel in which float an assortment of ingredients such as plump fresh shrimp, shreds of tart pickled vegetables, scallions, crisply fried tofu (bean curd), or croutons. Some Thais prefer to stir chopped-up salted duck egg into their *khao tom*, while others choose to break a raw egg into the hot soup, which poaches gently while they eat.

While many Thai soups are simple broth-and-noodle combinations, most menus highlight a few national classics. The sour and fiercely hot *tom yum*, with its tangy lime broth ablaze with chilies, and *tom kha*, the creamy combination of coconut milk and galangal, exemplify the two main flavor combinations the Thais enjoy in their soup bowls. Soup may be served as the first course or brought to the table in a tureen to eat with other main course dishes.

# MUSHROOMS IN GINGER SHRED SOUP

SERVES 6

YOUNG GINGER IS NEEDED FOR THIS DELICATELY FLAVORED SOUP. IDENTIFY IT BY ITS SMOOTH, CREAMY BUFF-COLORED SKIN AND PINK-TINGED BUDS; OLDER GINGER HAS WRINKLED SKIN OF A DEEPER BUFF-BEIGE HUE. IF YOU CAN ONLY OBTAIN OLDER GINGER, STEEP IT IN BOILING WATER FOR 1 TO 2 MINUTES TO REDUCE ITS PUNGENCY.

Place the dried fungus, dried mushrooms and 1½ cups of the water in a small saucepan and bring to a boil. Reduce the heat to medium-low and simmer gently, uncovered, until the mushrooms are very tender, about 20 minutes. Retrieve the fungus and mushrooms with a slotted spoon and set aside. Strain the mushroom liquid through a fine-mesh sieve into a medium-sized soup pot and add the vegetable stock and ginger.

If the black mushrooms have stems, trim them off close to the mushroom caps and discard. Trim off any woody parts from the fungus and shred it finely. Add the trimmed mushrooms, the shredded fungus, the straw mushrooms, and the golden, abalone, or oyster mushrooms to the soup. Bring almost to a boil, reducing the heat before the stock begins to bubble.

In a cup, mix together the cornstarch or arrowroot and the remaining ¼ cup water. Pour into the soup and stir until it becomes slightly thicker and translucent, about 3 minutes. Add the oyster sauce, and salt and white pepper. Ladle into deep bowls and garnish with basil or coriander.

¼ cup (½ ounce) shredded dried black (wood ear) fungus

6 dried black mushrooms

1¾ cups water

5 cups White Vegetable Stock (page 22)

2½ tablespoons finely shredded young fresh ginger (see introduction)

½ cup (3½ ounces) drained canned small straw mushrooms

½ cup (4 ounces) drained canned golden mushrooms or sliced abalone mushrooms, or 1 ounce small fresh oyster mushrooms

1½ tablespoons cornstarch or arrowroot

2 to 3 tablespoons vegetarian mushroom oyster sauce

Salt and white pepper, to taste

Shredded fresh basil leaves or coriander (cilantro)

# PUMPKIN AND COCONUT CREAM SOUP

SERVES 4 TO 6

**P**UMPKIN HAS A PARTICULAR AFFINITY WITH COCONUT CREAM, AND SO IS SUPERB IN COCONUT-BASED CURRIES AND SOUPS LIKE THIS ONE. GOLDEN SWEET POTATO IS EQUALLY AS GOOD. IF YOU CANNOT OBTAIN FRESH KAFFIR LIMES TO GARNISH THE SOUP, USE LIME ZEST IN ITS PLACE, TO FINISH THE SOUP WITH BRIGHT, CITRUS TASTE HIGHLIGHTS.

In a saucepan, combine the pumpkin, stock or water, ginger, and lemongrass. Cover, bring to a boil, reduce the heat to medium-low, and simmer until the pumpkin is very tender, about 12 minutes. Add the scallions and cook briefly.

Transfer the contents of the saucepan to a blender or food processor and process until the soup is partially pureed. Pour in half of the coconut cream and process until smooth.

Rinse the saucepan and pour the puree into it. Add half of the remaining coconut cream. Season with salt and pepper and heat through without allowing the soup to boil. Taste and adjust the seasoning and squeeze in lime or lemon juice.

If using the kaffir lime leaves, fold them in half and, using a sharp knife, trim away the hard central rib. Cut the leaves into threadlike shreds. Ladle the soup into bowls, add the remaining coconut cream, forming a swirl on top of each bowl, and garnish with the lime leaf or zest.

6 cups (1¾ pounds) peeled and cubed
   pumpkin

2 cups White Vegetable Stock (page 22)
   or water

½-inch piece fresh ginger, peeled

1 tablespoon chopped lemongrass

2 scallions, white parts only, finely sliced

2 cups coconut cream

1⅓ teaspoons salt

¼ teaspoon white pepper

Freshly squeezed lime or lemon juice, to
   taste

2 fresh kaffir lime leaves, or very finely
   shredded zest of 1 small fresh lime

# TOFU IN COCONUT SOUP WITH GALANGAL

SERVES 4 TO 6

THIS SOUP, **TOM TAO HOO KHA,** IS THE VEGETARIAN VERSION OF THE MUCH APPRECIATED **TOM KHA KAI,** CHICKEN AND THAI GINGER (GALANGAL) IN COCONUT SOUP. THE FRIED TOFU IS BEST ADDED AT THE LAST MINUTE, SO IT RETAINS SOME OF ITS CRUNCH. SOFT FRESH TOFU, CUT INTO ½-INCH CUBES, MAY BE USED INSTEAD.

2 kaffir lime leaves, lightly crushed

½ lemongrass stalk, bruised and halved
   lengthwise

1½-inch piece fresh galangal or young ginger

1 large, fresh mild red chili, seeded and
   coarsely chopped

2½ cups coconut cream

2 cups White Vegetable Stock (page 22)

½ to 1½ teaspoons Red Curry Paste
   (page 14)

1 cup vegetable oil

6 ounces fried or firm tofu (bean curd),
   cut into ½-inch cubes

Handful of fresh basil leaves

1 or 2 large, mild fresh red chilies, seeded
   and finely shredded

1½ ounces fresh small oyster mushrooms, or ½ cup (4 ounces) drained
   canned golden mushrooms

2 tablespoons fish sauce, or 1 tablespoon
   light soy sauce

Salt, to taste

Freshly squeezed lime or lemon juice, to
   taste

Place the lime leaves, lemongrass, galangal or ginger, chili, coconut cream, and stock in a soup pot. Bring to a boil, reduce the heat immediately to medium-low and stir in the curry paste. Simmer for about 6 minutes, until the soup is well flavored.

Meanwhile, heat the vegetable oil in a wok or deep skillet over medium-high heat. Rinse, drain and dry the fried tofu, if using. Add the fried or firm tofu to the oil, and fry until it is crisp and golden on all surfaces, about 3 minutes. Remove with a slotted spoon and set aside to drain on paper towels. Next, fry the basil leaves until they are crisp, about 45 seconds. Remove to paper towels to drain. Put the chili shreds into the oil and fry until crisp, about 1 minute. Remove to paper towels and discard the oil. Reserve the basil and chili for garnish.

Add the mushrooms to the soup and season with fish sauce or soy sauce, salt, and lime or lemon juice. Simmer until the mushrooms are heated through.

Divide the fried tofu among 4 to 6 small soup bowls. Ladle in the soup, distributing the mushrooms evenly. Float the fried basil leaves and chili shreds on the surface and serve immediately.

# HOT AND SOUR SOUP WITH BEAN THREAD VERMICELLI, TOMATO AND BASIL

**T**HAIS LOVE SOUPS WITH BOLD FLAVORS. THIS SOUP SHOULD BE HOT, PLEASINGLY TART, AND VERY AROMATIC FROM THE LAST-MINUTE ADDITION OF BASIL LEAVES.

Drain the vermicelli and place in a saucepan with the stock and *nam prik pow* sauce. Place over high heat and bring almost to a boil, then reduce the heat to medium-low. Add the bamboo shoots and radish or melon and simmer for 3 minutes. Add the bell pepper, chilies, and tomatoes, and season with the sugar and the fish sauce or use the soy sauce and yellow bean sauce. Again bring the soup just below a boil, and simmer for about 2 minutes.

In a small bowl, stir together the cornstarch and water. Pour into the soup, and stir until it thickens slightly, about 2 minutes. Taste and adjust the seasoning. Stir in the basil leaves and ladle the soup into bowls. Add a sprinkle of chili-flavored vinegar to each bowl. Pass the remaining vinegar at the table.

NOTE: *Sambal ulek* or fresh chilies ground to a paste with a little salt can be substituted for the *nam prik pow* sauce.

VARIATIONS: Beat 1 or 2 eggs, and pour slowly into the finished hot soup in a thin stream, so the egg sets in fine threads. To serve the soup as a main course, add 3 or 4 ounces soft tofu (bean curd) cut into small cubes to the finished soup and heat for about 1 minute.

*1½ ounces bean thread vermicelli (wun see), soaked in hot water to cover for 15 minutes*

*6 cups White Vegetable Stock (page 22)*

*1 teaspoon Vegetarian Nam Prik Pow Sauce (page 16; see note)*

*¼ cup (1¼ ounces) matchstick-cut bamboo shoots*

*¼ cup (1 ounce) matchstick-cut Japanese white radish or Chinese melon*

*¼ green bell pepper, seeded and finely sliced*

*1 to 2 large, mild fresh red chilies, seeded and finely shredded*

*2 firm small tomatoes, cut into wedges, or 6 cherry tomatoes, cut in half*

*1 tablespoon superfine white sugar*

*¼ cup fish sauce, or 1 tablespoon light soy sauce and 1 tablespoon smoothly mashed yellow bean sauce*

*1 tablespoon cornstarch*

*½ cup water*

*¾ cup loosely packed fresh basil leaves*

*¼ cup distilled white vinegar or Chinese red vinegar, mixed with 1 teaspoon minced fresh red chili*

# SPICY CREAMED TARO AND PEANUT SOUP

SERVES 6

TARO IS AN EXCELLENT VEGETABLE TO INCLUDE IN A VEGETARIAN DIET, AS IT HAS A MEATY TEXTURE THAT IS PLEASING TO THE PALATE. IT MASHES SMOOTHLY, ABSORBS FLAVORS READILY, AND CRISPS SUPERBLY WHEN FRIED. WHEN PEELING TARO, CUT RIGHT DOWN TO THE GRAY-PINK FLESH, AND NEVER TASTE IT UNCOOKED. RAW TARO CONTAINS AN ENZYME THAT CAN BURN THE LIPS AND CAUSE YOUR THROAT TO SWELL. THIS SMOOTH AND VELVETY SOUP IS ALSO GOOD MADE WITH GOLDEN SWEET POTATO.

½ cup peanut or peanut oil

1 leek, carefully washed and finely
  sliced, or 1 yellow onion, finely sliced

4 garlic cloves, crushed

¼ cup finely shredded young fresh ginger

1 to 3 mild, fresh red chilies, seeded and
  minced

1½ to 1¾ pounds taro, thickly peeled

¾ cup (3¼ ounces) unsalted roasted
  peanuts (see note)

2 to 3 teaspoons Red Curry Paste (page 14)

6 cups White Vegetable Stock (page 22)

½ cup sliced scallions, white and half the
  green

1¼ tablespoons medium palm sugar or
  soft brown sugar

Freshly squeezed lime or lemon juice, to taste

Salt and freshly ground black pepper, to taste

½ to ¾ cup coconut cream

2 tablespoons chopped unsalted roasted
  peanuts or Crisp-Fried Shallots
  (page 24), for garnish

Finely sliced scallion greens, for garnish

In a soup pot over medium heat, warm the oil. Add the leek or onion, garlic, ginger, and chilies. Cover and "sweat," shaking the pan from time to time to turn the ingredients and prevent them from sticking, until wilted, 5 to 6 minutes.

Meanwhile, cut four-fifths of the taro into ⅓-inch cubes, and cut the remainder into 1-inch chunks.

Uncover the pot, add the cubed taro and taro chunks, the peanuts, and curry paste. Raise the heat slightly. Cook for 5 minutes, stirring frequently. Pour in the stock and bring to a boil over high heat. Reduce the heat to medium and simmer until the taro is tender, about 15 minutes.

Add the scallions, sugar, lime or lemon juice, salt, and pepper. Stir well and simmer for a few minutes over low heat. Using tongs, remove the chunks of taro and set them aside. Pour half of the contents of the soup pot into a food processor or blender and process to a puree. Pour into a clean saucepan. Puree the remaining soup in the same way and add to the first batch.

Cut the reserved taro into small cubes and place in the soup. Add the coconut cream and heat gently to serving temperature. Ladle into deep bowls and garnish with the peanuts or shallots and the scallion greens.

NOTE: If only salted roasted peanuts can be found, rinse in water and dry well before using.

# EGG SHREDS AND WATER SPINACH IN CLEAR SOUP

SERVES 6 TO 8

W ATER SPINACH, MORE CORRECTLY WATER CONVOLVULUS, IS CALLED **PAK BUNG** IN THAILAND, BUT ELSEWHERE IN SOUTHEAST ASIA IT IS MORE COMMONLY KNOWN AS **KANGKUNG**. IT HAS LONG, HOLLOW STEMS ON WHICH GROW SLENDER, TAPERING LEAVES THAT TASTE LIKE SPINACH, WHICH CAN BE USED IN ITS PLACE.

In a bowl, beat the eggs until blended. Add a pinch of salt and set aside. In a wok or nonstick skillet over high heat, warm the oil. Add the garlic and fry until well browned, about 40 seconds. Remove the garlic and discard.

Using the same oil, pour in half of the beaten egg, tilting the pan so it spreads evenly. As soon as it begins cooking, add 1 tablespoon of the scallions, scattering them on evenly. Reduce the heat to medium and cook the egg until golden on the underside, about 2 minutes, then turn and cook the other side until golden, about 1½ minutes longer. When cooked, remove to a plate to cool. Increase the heat to high before pouring the remaining egg into the pan, then reduce to medium again and cook in the same way, adding another 1 tablespoon of the scallions. Remove and set aside to cool.

Bring a small saucepan of water to a boil, add the bean sprouts, and blanch for 20 seconds. Transfer to a colander to drain, and set aside. When the egg crêpes are cool, roll them up into cylinders, and cut crosswise into fine strips.

In a saucepan, combine the stock and ginger, and bring almost to a boil. Add the corn and spinach and cook for about 4 minutes. Add the bean sprouts and shredded egg and heat briefly.

Season the soup with the fish sauce or soy sauce, the oyster sauce, and salt and pepper. Ladle into bowls, scatter on the remaining scallions, and serve.

2 small eggs

Salt

2 teaspoons vegetable oil

1 large garlic clove, finely chopped

3 tablespoons minced scallions, white and some greens

1 cup (3 ounces) bean sprouts

6 cups White Vegetable Stock (page 22)

2 teaspoons minced or grated fresh ginger

⅓ cup (1½ ounces) corn kernels

1½ cups (4 ounces) loosely packed water spinach leaves

1 tablespoon fish sauce, or 2 teaspoons light soy sauce

2 tablespoons vegetarian mushroom oyster sauce

White pepper, to taste

# MUSHROOMS IN COCONUT SOUP WITH CRISP NOODLE CROUTONS

CRISP AND CRUNCHY CROUTONS MADE FROM STRIPS OF FRIED WONTON WRAPPERS, PROVIDE A PLEASING TEXTURAL CONTRAST TO THIS SMOOTH AND CREAMY SOUP.

1½ cups coconut cream

1½ cups White Vegetable Stock
   (page 22) or water

1 lemongrass stalk, trimmed and slit in
   half lengthwise

3 kaffir lime leaves

1-inch piece fresh galangal, or ½-inch
   piece fresh ginger

2 scallions, white parts only, chopped

½ to ¾ teaspoon Red Curry Paste
   (page 14)

1 cup (7 ounces) drained canned small
   straw mushrooms (see notes)

1½ tablespoons fish sauce (see notes)

Salt and white pepper, to taste

2 teaspoons cornstarch

¼ cup water

2 fresh coriander (cilantro) sprigs, chopped

For the Croutons

6 fresh or frozen wonton skins (wrappers), placed in warm part of kitchen
   to soften for 20 minutes if frozen

1 cup peanut or vegetable oil

Salt

In a saucepan, combine the coconut cream, stock or water, and lemongrass. Bruise the kaffir lime leaves by crushing them firmly in your hand, to release their aroma. Peel and very thinly slice the galangal or ginger. Add the kaffir lime leaves, galangal or ginger, the chili, if using, and scallions to the pan and bring the soup to a boil over high heat. Reduce the heat to medium-low and add the curry paste. Simmer for 5 minutes, then add the straw mushrooms and the fish sauce or the soy sauce and the fermented tofu and brine. Season to taste with salt and pepper and simmer for 2 to 3 minutes.

In a small bowl, stir together the cornstarch and water and pour into the soup. Raise the heat slightly and simmer, stirring, until the soup thickens slightly. Add the coriander and reduce heat to very low to keep warm.

Meanwhile, make the croutons. Cut the wonton skins into ½-inch-wide strips. Pour the oil into a wok or deep pan and place over high heat. When the oil is hot, add the wonton skin strips and fry until crisp and golden, about 40 seconds. Remove with a slotted spoon and drain on paper towels. Sprinkle lightly with salt.

Discard the lemongrass and lime leaves from the soup and ladle the soup into bowls. Garnish each serving with the croutons and a sprinkle of coriander. Serve at once.

NOTES: If only large straw mushrooms are available, thinly slice them. For a vegetarian alternative to fish sauce, use 1 teaspoon light soy sauce, 2½ to 3 teaspoons brine from fermented tofu (bean curd), and ½ teaspoon smoothly mashed fermented tofu.

# CLASSIC THAI RICE SOUP

SERVES 4

IN THAILAND, RICE SOUP, OR **KHAO TOM**, IS RARELY SERVED WITH A MEAL. IT'S A CLEVER WAY TO USE UP LEFTOVER RICE, AND IS THEREFORE A POPULAR BREAKFAST OR SNACK DISH. SALTED VEGETABLES, TOFU, AND WATER SPINACH GO INTO THIS VEGETARIAN VERSION, WHILE NONVEGETARIANS ENJOY THE SOUP WITH BIG FRESH SHRIMP, SLIVERS OF CHICKEN OR PORK, A SPRINKLE OF CHOPPED SCALLIONS, AND A RAW EGG.

6 ounces firm tofu (bean curd)

1 cup peanut or vegetable oil

3 large garlic cloves, thinly sliced

8 cups White Vegetable Stock (page 22)

2½ cups cooked jasmine or other long-grain white rice (see note)

2 to 3 ounces small spinach leaves, stems removed

⅓ cup (1¼ ounces) small fresh oyster mushrooms, or ¼ cup (1¾ ounces) drained canned button or straw mushrooms

2 to 4 tablespoons fish sauce or light soy sauce

Salt and white pepper, to taste

1¼ tablespoons salt-pickled radish or mustard greens, minced

Chopped fresh coriander (cilantro)

8 lime wedges

1 or 2 hot fresh red chilies, seeded and chopped

Cut the tofu into thin slices 1½ inches long by ¾ inch wide. In a wok or skillet over medium-high heat, warm the oil. When hot, add the tofu and fry, turning as necessary, until golden brown and crisped on the surface, about 4 minutes. Retrieve with a slotted spoon and place on paper towels to drain.

Pour off all but 3 tablespoons of the oil from the pan and place the pan over medium heat. Add the garlic and fry, turning almost continually, until golden brown, about 3 minutes. Remove with a slotted spoon and drain on paper towels. Reserve both the garlic and the garlic oil.

Meanwhile, pour the stock into a saucepan and add the rice. Bring to a boil, then reduce the heat to medium. Simmer until the rice begins to break up, 10 to 20 minutes. Add the spinach and mushrooms and the fish sauce or soy sauce. Simmer to heat through and blend the flavors, 2 to 3 minutes. Season with salt and pepper.

Divide the salt-pickled vegetables and the fried tofu among 4 large bowls. Ladle the soup into the bowls, dividing evenly. Scatter on the fried garlic and the coriander. Add about 2 teaspoons of the reserved garlic oil to each bowl. Serve with lime wedges and chili for diners to add to taste.

N O T E : You will need to cook 1 cup raw long-grain white rice to yield 2½ cups cooked rice.

V A R I A T I O N : Break a raw egg into each bowl of soup just before serving. At the table, the egg is stirred into the hot soup.

# VEGETABLES IN HOT ORANGE CURRY SOUP

SERVES 6 TO 8

**T**HAI ORANGE CURRIES HAVE A UNIQUE FLAVOR AND COLOR DUE TO THE USE OF TWO INGREDIENTS, VINEGAR FOR TARTNESS AND DRIED RED CHILIES AND THE STRONGLY COLORED OUTER LAYERS OF ONION OR SHALLOT FOR COLOR. MAKE NO MISTAKE: THIS IS HOT IF YOU USE ALL THE CHILIES GIVEN IN THE CURRY PASTE RECIPE.

To make the curry paste, soak the chilies in boiling water to cover for 15 minutes. Remove the chilies from their soaking water and chop finely. Place the chilies (including a little of the soaking water), shallots, bean sauce, garlic, and vinegar in a mortar, spice grinder, or blender. Pound or grind to a smooth paste, adding more of the water as needed. Set aside.

To make the soup, pour the water into a large saucepan and add the sweet potato or taro and the pumpkin. Bring to a boil, reduce the heat to medium-low, and simmer for 10 minutes. Add the chayote or melon, radish, and eggplant and cook until they are almost tender, about 10 minutes longer.

Add the orange curry paste, cabbage, and tamarind concentrate or lemon juice, and simmer until the cabbage is tender, about 6 minutes. Stir in the coconut cream, the fish sauce or soy sauce, the sugar, and lime or lemon juice. Heat briefly, then check the seasonings and adjust to taste. The soup should be thick, hot, and tart. Stir in the coriander or basil leaves.

Ladle into soup bowls and serve.

NOTES: If you can't find tamarind, you can substitute 2 to 3 teaspoons freshly squeezed lemon juice. Superfine white sugar can be used for light palm sugar. Shredded coconut or chopped unsalted roasted peanuts make a nice garnish for this soup.

## For the Curry Paste
*2 to 4 large dried red chilies, seeded*

*3 red shallots or salad onion*

*2 teaspoons yellow bean sauce*

*1 large garlic clove*

*1½ teaspoons white or rice vinegar*

## For the Soup
*6 cups water*

*⅓ cup (1½ ounces) peeled and diced
    sweet potato or taro*

*⅓ cup (1½ ounces) peeled and diced pumpkin*

*⅓ cup (1¼ ounces) peeled and diced
    chayote or Chinese melon*

*⅓ cup (1¼ ounces) peeled and diced
    Japanese white radish*

*½ cup (2 ounces) unpeeled, diced eggplant*

*1½ cups (4½ ounces) chopped Chinese cabbage*

*1 teaspoon tamarind (see note)*

*1 cup coconut cream*

*1½ tablespoons fish sauce or light soy sauce*

*Light palm or white sugar, to taste*

*Freshly squeezed lime or lemon juice, to taste*

*2 tablespoons chopped coriander, or 8
    basil leaves, shredded*

# SALADS

THAI SALADS ARE HEROIC COMBINATIONS OF MANY DIFFERENT INGREDIENTS, CHOSEN FOR THEIR COLOR, TASTE AND TEXTURAL INTEREST. They feature flavors that zing on the palate, textures that crunch or slip easily over the tongue, ingredients that suprise and delight. Fresh greens, bean sprouts, cucumbers, peppers, celery, red and yellow onions, scallions, shallots, garlic chives, slender leeks, and noodles are all salad basics. Wild mushrooms, bamboo shoots, water chestnuts, and many native fruits are among the more exotic additions. Thai salad dressings are tart, sweet, hot, and salty from a mix of citrus juices, palm sugar, chilies, and fish sauce; nutty from the presence of roasted peanuts or sesame seeds; aromatic from a generous use of fresh herbs.

The role of the Thai salad in a meal is equally versatile. It can be served as a lightweight lunch dish or a first course on individual plates. More traditionally, it is offered as a kind of intermezzo between the first and main courses, or midway through an extensive menu of main dishes.

# CUCUMBER SALAD WITH ROASTED PEANUT DRESSING

SERVES 4 TO 8

THAI CUISINE FEATURES MANY SALADS, USING FRESH AND COOKED VEGETABLES, AND EVEN FRUIT. DRESSINGS ARE PALATE-STIMULATING BLENDS OF TART, HOT, SWEET, AND PUNGENT TASTES IN WHICH LIME JUICE, CHILIES, FISH SAUCE AND SHRIMP PASTE, AND PALM SUGAR INVARIABLY FEATURE. FINELY CHOPPED ROASTED PEANUTS, FRESH BASIL AND CORIANDER, AND KAFFIR LIME OR LEMONGRASS ARE THE OTHER KEY FLAVOR ELEMENTS OF THAI SALADS.

Peel the cucumbers, then cut off the flesh in thick strips, discarding the seed core. Cut the flesh into strips the size of a matchstick. Cut the bell pepper into strips of similar size. Mix the cucumber and pepper strips in a salad bowl.

Parboil the green beans in lightly salted boiling water for 2 minutes. Retrieve with a slotted spoon and refresh in ice water. Blanch the bean sprouts for 20 seconds in the same boiling water, drain, and refresh in ice water. Drain beans and bean sprouts and add to the cucumber and pepper strips along with the coriander, basil, scallion greens, and the peanuts. Mix the ingredients together thoroughly.

To make the dressing, in a small bowl, whisk together the lime or lemon juice, sugar, garlic, and chili. Finely chop the peanuts and stir into the dressing. Pour over the salad and toss to mix. Line a serving plate with lettuce leaves and spoon the salad over the leaves.

VARIATION: Use roasted cashew nuts instead of peanuts.

1¼ pounds cucumber

⅓ red bell pepper, seeded

½ cup (2 ounces) sliced green beans, (1½-inch pieces)

1¼ cups (4 ounces) bean sprouts

½ cup loosely packed fresh coriander (cilantro) leaves

¼ cup loosely packed shredded fresh basil leaves

¼ cup chopped scallion greens

⅓ cup (1½ ounces) chopped unsalted roasted peanuts

For the Dressing

⅓ cup freshly squeezed lime or lemon juice

1½ tablespoons medium-light palm sugar or soft brown sugar

1 large garlic clove, crushed

1 mild or hot fresh red chili, seeded and finely shredded

1 tablespoon unsalted roasted peanuts

Lettuce leaves

# SWEET AND SOUR POMELO SALAD

SERVES 4 TO 6

**T**HIS IS ONE OF THE MOST POPULAR SALADS IN THAILAND, WHERE IT IS CALLED **YAM SOM OH**. POME-LOS ARE LARGE CITRUS FRUITS RESEMBLING GRAPEFRUITS, ALTHOUGH LESS JUICY. COMMON OR PINK GRAPEFRUITS CAN BE PREPARED IN THE SAME WAY, OR WHOLE TANGERINE OR ORANGE SEGMENTS CAN BE SUBSTITUTED. THE SWEETER FRUITS MAY REQUIRE SOME ADJUSTMENT TO THE DRESSING, TO ACHIEVE A BALANCE OF SWEET AND SOUR FLAVORS.

*1 cup peanut or vegetable oil*

*¾ cup (3 ounces) cubed tempeh (see note) or firm tofu (bean curd)*

*1 cup (3 ounces) shaved fresh coconut meat, or 1 cup (2 ounces) flaked dried coconut*

*2 pomelos, 3 grapefruits, or 4 or 5 tangerines, about 1¼ pounds total weight*

For the Dressing

*3 tablespoons coconut cream*

*1 to 1½ teaspoons Vegetarian Nam Prik Pow Sauce (page 16)*

*2 tablespoons fish sauce, or 1½ tablespoons light (thin) soy sauce*

*1 tablespoon freshly squeezed lime juice*

*2 teaspoons light palm or white sugar*

*1 small red onion, finely sliced*

*2 to 4 small, mild fresh red or green chilies, seeded and finely chopped*

*1 tablespoon Crisp-Fried Shallots (page 24)*

*Lettuce leaves*

In a wok or skillet over medium heat, heat the oil. Add the tempeh, tofu, or vegetarian bacon and fry, turning from time to time, until crisp, about 2½ minutes. Remove with a slotted spoon to paper towels to drain. Add the coconut to the oil remaining in the pan and fry over medium heat, stirring almost continuously, until barely golden, about 5 minutes. Remove with a slotted spoon to paper towels to drain. Discard the oil.

Peel the pomelos or other fruit and divide into segments. Tear the pomelo and grapefruit segments into smaller pieces; leave the orange or tangerine segments whole. Place in a salad bowl and add the coconut and tempeh, tofu or "bacon."

To make the dressing, in a saucepan, combine the coconut cream and *nam prik pow* sauce and place over medium-high heat until it begins to bubble. Reduce the heat to medium-low and simmer gently until the mixture has reduced a little, about 5 minutes. Remove from the heat and let cool, then add the fish sauce or soy sauce, lime or lemon juice, and sugar. Stir until the sugar dissolves and the flavors are well blended.

Pour the dressing over the citrus mixture and add the onion, chilies, and shallots. Toss lightly. Line a serving plate with lettuce leaves and spoon the salad over the top.

NOTE: Vegetarian bacon, finely sliced, can be added or substituted for tempeh. Coriander (cilantro) and mint add wonderful fresh flavors to the salad. Garnish generously with these chopped, fresh herbs.

# GREEN PAPAYA SALAD

SERVES 6

**G**REEN PAPAYA SALAD, CALLED **SOM TAM**, IS A CLASSIC SALAD FROM THE NORTH. IT MAKES A FLAVORFUL ACCOMPANIMENT TO JUST ABOUT ANY THAI DISH. IT'S ALSO A GREAT WAY TO INTRODUCE A THAI MENU, OFFERING IT AS THE FIRST COURSE. SERVE IN A CUP-SHAPED LETTUCE OR CHINESE CABBAGE LEAF, WITH PERHAPS A SMALL SERVING OF FRIED TOFU (PAGE 55) TOPPED WITH SWEET CHILI SAUCE ON THE SIDE. UNRIPE MANGO CAN BE SUBSTITUTED FOR THE PAPAYA.

*1 unripened papaya (½ pound), peeled
   and seeded*
*2 large garlic cloves*
*1 tablespoon unsalted roasted peanuts*
*2 to 3 tablespoons Vegetarian Nam Jim
   Sauce (page 17)*
*½ cup (2 ounces) sliced long beans or
   green beans (1-inch pieces)*
*1 large ripe tomato, cut into wedges*
*¼ cup sliced scallion greens*
*1 teaspoon Roasted Chili Powder
   (page 13)*
*Lettuce leaves*

For the Garnish
*Decorative chili strips or chili flowers
   (page 25)*
*Fresh coriander (cilantro) sprigs or
   scallion curls (page 25)*

Coarsely grate the papaya into a bowl. In a mortar or large food processor, combine the garlic and peanuts and pound or grind to a paste. Add the papaya and pound briefly or pulse until the papaya is broken up but not pulverized. Add the *nam jim* sauce and pound or pulse again briefly.

At this point, you can choose how you prefer to continue with the recipe. Traditionally, the beans and tomato are pounded with the salad. This releases their juices and integrates their flavors, but does not make for a visually appealing finished dish. If you prefer, simply add raw sliced beans (or parboil them in lightly salted water for 2 minutes and refresh in ice water), tomato wedges, and the sliced scallions. Season with the chili powder and toss together.

Line a serving plate with lettuce leaves and spoon the salad on top. Garnish with the chili strips or flowers and the coriander or scallion curls.

# VEGETARIAN LAAB

SERVES 4

LIKE MOST THAI SALADS, THIS MAKES A GOOD FIRST COURSE. IT IS DRESSED WITH HOT AND CRUNCHY GRANULES OF ROASTED WHITE RICE AND CHILI. IF YOU PREFER TO AVOID CHILI HEAT, SUBSTITUTE FINELY CHOPPED ROASTED PEANUTS, CASHEWS, OR PINE NUTS FOR THE RICE AND CHILI MIXTURE.

Place the rice and chilies in a wok or skillet without oil and place over medium-high heat. Cook, stirring frequently, until the rice is golden brown and the chilies have turned a deep red, about 4 minutes. Shake the pan frequently to help turn the rice and chilies so they cook evenly. Remove to a mortar or spice grinder and let cool. Rinse and thoroughly dry the wok or skillet.

Cut the tofu into ⅓-inch cubes. Pour the oil into the wok or skillet and place over high heat. Add the tofu and fry, turning and stirring with a flat spoon as needed, until golden and crisped on the edges, about 8 minutes. Remove with a slotted spoon, draining well over the pan, and spread on a plate. Set aside for a few minutes to cool.

Pour off all but 1¼ tablespoons of the oil from the pan and place the pan over medium-high heat. Add the chopped onion and cook, stirring frequently, until deep brown, about 3½ minutes. Remove from the heat.

In a bowl, combine the tofu, fried onion, lemongrass or citrus zest, sliced onion, bell pepper, and half of the mint or basil.

Grind the rice and chilies until they are the texture of coarse sand. Sprinkle about 2 teaspoons over the salad, reserving some for garnishing. Add the fish sauce or soy sauce and salt and the sugar to the salad and mix well. Then add the remaining mint or basil.

Line a serving plate with lettuce leaves, if using. Mound the salad on top, and sprinkle on a teaspoon or two of the ground rice and chili (unused rice and chili granules can be kept in a spice jar on the shelf for several months). Serve with lime wedges.

1½ tablespoons long-grain white rice

2 to 3 dried red chilies, seeded

1 pound firm tofu (bean curd)

2 cups peanut or vegetable oil

½ cup (2 ounces) finely chopped yellow onion

⅓ cup very, very finely sliced lemongrass, or 1 tablespoon finely shredded lemon or lime zest

1 red onion, finely sliced

1 small red bell pepper, seeded and finely sliced

1 cup loosely packed small fresh mint or sweet basil leaves

2 to 3 tablespoons fish sauce, or 2 tablespoons light soy sauce and salt, to taste

Superfine white sugar, to taste

Lettuce leaves (optional)

Lime wedges

# ASPARAGUS AND BEAN SPROUT SALAD

SERVES 4 TO 6

**W**HEN FRESH ASPARAGUS IS OUT OF SEASON, I USE ABOUT 8 OUNCES LONG BEANS OR GREEN BEANS, CUT INTO 2-INCH PIECES, WHOLE SNOW PEAS, OR SMALL BROCCOLI FLORETS IN THEIR PLACE.

Trim off the tough ends of the asparagus stems, then slice on the diagonal into 1-inch pieces. Bring a pan of lightly salted water to a boil, add the asparagus, and parboil for 2 minutes. Remove with a slotted spoon and refresh in ice water. Drain thoroughly and place in a salad bowl.

Blanch the bean sprouts in the same boiling water for 20 seconds, drain, and refresh in ice water, then drain again thoroughly. Add to the asparagus along with the shallot or onion, chili, and peanuts.

To make the dressing, whisk together all the ingredients until well blended. Pour over the salad and toss lightly to mix.

Line a serving plate with the lettuce leaves and mound the salad on top. Surround with the egg wedges, if using. Scatter on the chili shreds and serve.

8 to 12 fresh asparagus spears

2½ cups (8 ounces) bean sprouts

3 shallots or 1 red onion, finely sliced

1 fresh hot red chili, seeded and finely sliced (optional)

2½ tablespoons unsalted roasted peanuts, chopped

For the Dressing

½ cup coconut cream

1 tablespoon light soy sauce

3 tablespoons freshly squeezed lime or lemon juice

½ teaspoon salt

1 tablespoon light palm sugar or superfine white sugar

1 tablespoon Sweet Chili Sauce (page 18)

1 teaspoon finely grated lime zest

2 teaspoons minced fresh coriander (cilantro)

For Serving

Lettuce leaves

Hard-cooked eggs, cut into wedges (optional)

Fresh red chili shreds

# ROASTED EGGPLANT SALAD

SERVES 4 TO 6

THAI SALADS ARE ALWAYS A SURPRISE. THE MIX OF INGREDIENTS IS UNUSUAL, THE DRESSINGS A HEADY BLEND OF MANY FLAVORS. THIS SALAD OF ROASTED EGGPLANT AND CUCUMBER, WHICH IN THAILAND IS NAMED **YAM MAKUA YAO**, IS TYPICAL. THE RECIPE IS A SCALED-DOWN VERSION OF A SALAD I HAD ONCE IN CHIANG MAI, WHICH INCLUDED CRINKLY, CRUNCHY WHITE FUNGUS AND SHREDS OF CRISP BLACK FUNGUS.

*1¼ pounds slender Asian eggplants*

*½ cup (2 ounces) unsalted roasted peanuts*

*1½ cups (5 to 6 ounces) cubed, unpeeled cucumber*

*3 tablespoons peanut or vegetable oil*

*½ cup finely sliced scallions, white and some greens, plus sliced greens for garnish*

*1 or 2 mild fresh green chilies, seeded and minced*

*1 to 2 tablespoons chopped fresh coriander (cilantro) leaves and stems*

For the Dressing:

*3 tablespoons freshly squeezed lime or lemon juice*

*1 tablespoon fish sauce, or 2 to 3 teaspoons light (thin) soy sauce*

*1½ to 2 teaspoons superfine white sugar*

Prepare a fire in a charcoal grill, preheat a broiler, or preheat an oven to 360 degrees F. Place the eggplants on a grill rack or broiler rack about 4 inches from the fire or the broiler heat, or place in a roasting dish and put into the oven. Cook until soft, turning once or twice so the eggplants brown evenly, until they are soft to the touch with darkly charred skin, about 20 minutes. Alternatively, roast the eggplants by placing them directly over a gas flame on the stove top, and cook, using tongs to turn them frequently, until soft and well charred.

Remove the eggplants from the grill, broiler, oven, or gas flame, place them in a brown paper or plastic bag, and close the bag. The steam trapped inside will help loosen their skins, making the eggplants easier to peel. Set aside for a few minutes to cool. Peel the eggplants, and then cut the flesh into chunks. Place in a bowl and add two-thirds of the peanuts, the cucumber, the oil, the ½ cup scallions, the chilies, and the coriander, and mix gently.

In a small bowl, make the dressing. Combine the lime juice, fish sauce, and sugar, and mix well. Pour over the salad and again mix gently. Transfer to a serving bowl. Chop the remaining peanuts and scatter them over the salad along with the scallion greens. Serve at once.

VARIATION: Blanched bean sprouts or strips of fresh or roasted red pepper can be added to the salad.

# EGG CRÊPE SALAD

SERVES 4 TO 6

EGGS ARE IMPORTANT TO MOST ASIAN CUISINES, AND THEY ARE USED IN MANY ORIGINAL WAYS. THREADS OF FINELY SHREDDED, TISSUE-THIN EGG CRÊPES ARE DRAPED OVER MANY POPULAR THAI DISHES AS A GARNISH. THICKER CRÊPES, SLICED OR CHOPPED, ARE USED AS A MAIN INGREDIENT IN CURRIES AND SALADS. THIS SALAD, KNOWN AS **YAM KAI KEEM** IN THAILAND, IS TYPICAL.

In a bowl, beat together the eggs, salt and pepper, and coriander; set aside. Blanch the bean sprouts in lightly salted boiling water for 15 seconds. Drain and refresh in ice water, then drain again. Cut the bell peppers or chilies into matchstick strips. Combine the bean sprouts, bell or chili peppers, celery, white or red onion, and mint leaves in a bowl. Separate lettuce leaves and tear large ones into smaller pieces. Add to the salad, cover with plastic wrap, and refrigerate until needed.

Place a small wok or nonstick skillet over medium-high heat and moisten with a little of the oil. Pour in one-fourth of the beaten eggs, and tilt the pan and swirl the egg so it forms an even, round shape. Cook until golden on the underside, about 45 seconds, then flip over and cook the other side until golden, about 35 seconds. Remove to a plate. Cook the remaining beaten eggs in the same way, to make 4 egg crêpes in all. Set aside to cool while preparing the dressing.

To make the dressing, in a small bowl, whisk together all the dressing ingredients. Taste and adjust the seasonings. The dressing should be slightly salty, with a hint of sweetness and evident tartness.

Cut the egg crêpes into small wedges, or into strips 2 inches long by ½ inch wide. Add to the salad and mix gently. Add the dressing and toss lightly, then serve.

NOTES: To reduce the pungency of the onion, blanch in boiling water for 20 seconds, then drain and refresh in ice water. Drain again and dry in a kitchen towel. Large, mild red or green chilies would replace bell peppers in Thailand.

## For the Salad

5 eggs

Salt and white pepper, to taste

2 tablespoons minced fresh coriander

1 cup (3 ounces) bean sprouts

¼ red bell pepper, seeded (see notes)

¼ green bell pepper, seeded (see notes)

1 cup (4 ounces) thinly sliced celery

½ cup finely sliced white or red onion
    (see notes)

¾ cup loosely packed mint leaves

1 small head romaine lettuce

2 teaspoons peanut or vegetable oil

## For the Dressing

1 garlic clove, minced

1 small, hot fresh red or green chili,
    seeded and minced

2 tablespoons freshly squeezed lime juice

2 tablespoons fish sauce, or 1½ table-
    spoons light soy sauce

1½ teaspoons superfine white sugar, to taste

2 tablespoons peeled and finely grated carrot

1 tablespoon unsalted roasted peanuts, minced

Salt and white pepper, to taste

# HOT AND SOUR TOFU SALAD

SERVES 4 TO 6

CHOOSE THE FRESHEST SOFT TOFU YOU CAN OBTAIN FOR THIS DELICIOUSLY APPETIZING SALAD, AND HANDLE IT WITH DELICACY. IN THAILAND, COOKS USE THE PEPPERY HERBS THAT GROW WILD ON THE BANKS OF **KLONGS** (CANALS) AND RIVERS FOR SALADS LIKE THIS. ARUGULA IS A PERFECT SUBSTITUTE.

*1 pound soft tofu (bean curd)*

*2 small bunches arugula*

*¾ cup loosely packed fresh herb leaves*
*    such as mint, basil, chervil, Japanese*
*    mitsuba, or coriander (cilantro), in*
*    any combination*

For the Dressing

*4 red shallots, thinly sliced, or 1 small*
*    red onion, sliced*

*2 scallions, white and some greens, finely*
*    sliced*

*2 fresh kaffir lime leaves, very very*
*    finely sliced (optional)*

*2 tablespoons freshly squeezed lime or*
*    lemon juice*

*2 tablespoons fish sauce, or 1 tablespoon*
*    light soy sauce*

*1 teaspoon Vegetarian Nam Prik Pow*
*    sauce (page 16)*

*1 tablespoon very, very finely minced*
*    lemongrass*

*1½ teaspoons superfine white sugar*

*Salt, to taste*

The best way to cut soft tofu is to hold a piece in the palm of your hand, and carefully cut it into 1-inch cubes with a serrated knife, taking care not to cut your palm. Arrange the arugula and half of the herbs on individual plates and place the bean curd cubes on top, dividing them evenly.

To make the dressing, in a bowl, briefly whisk together all the ingredients until well blended. Spoon the dressing evenly over the tofu and garnish with the remaining herbs. Serve at room temperature, or cover with plastic wrap and chill for 30 minutes before serving.

# VINEGAR·PICKLED VEGETABLES

MAKES 4 CUPS

**A**CRUNCHY SIDE DISH OF PICKLED VEGETABLES COMPLEMENTS JUST ABOUT ANY THAI MEAL. THIS RECIPE, CALLED **PAK DONG**, IS USEFUL TO HAVE ON HAND, SO I USUALLY MAKE UP A GENEROUS AMOUNT.

In a nonreactive saucepan such as stainless steel, enamel, or glass, combine the vinegar, water, sugar, and salt and bring to a boil, stirring to dissolve the sugar and salt. Add the prepared vegetables and ginger and boil until the vegetables are crisp-tender, about 4 minutes.

Meanwhile, in a small skillet over medium-high heat, warm the peanut oil and the sesame oil if using. Add the garlic, the onion or shallots, the chili, and the peppercorns and fry, stirring often, until they are all lightly browned, about 3 minutes.

Add the garlic mixture to the vegetables and simmer over medium-high heat for 2 minutes. Remove from the heat and pour into a heatproof glass or stainless-steel bowl. Let cool, then pack into clean jars. Cover and refrigerate for up to 2 weeks.

*1 cup distilled white vinegar or rice vinegar*

*½ cup water*

*3 to 4 tablespoons superfine white sugar*

*1 teaspoon salt*

*1 cup (4 ounces) sliced, unpeeled cucumber*

*1 cup (5 ounces) peeled and sliced carrot*

*1½ cups (5 ounces) small cauliflower florets*

*1 cup (3 ounces) cut-up Chinese cabbage (1-inch squares)*

*2 tablespoons finely shredded fresh ginger*

*1 tablespoon peanut oil*

*1 teaspoon sesame oil (optional)*

*4 garlic cloves, sliced*

*1 small red onion or 3 red shallots, sliced*

*1 medium-sized, hot fresh red chili, seeded and sliced*

*3 or 4 black peppercorns, lightly crushed*

# BEAN THREAD VERMICELLI SALAD

SERVES 4 TO 6

THIS DELIGHTFULLY CRUNCHY SALAD MAKES AN INTERESTING FIRST COURSE. THE CHOICE OF VEG-
ETABLES IS ARBITRARY. IN THAILAND, COOKS MIGHT USE JICAMA AND WINGED BEANS, AN UNUSUAL
BEAN WITH SQUARE-SHAPED SIDES, EACH EDGE OF WHICH IS EMBELLISHED WITH A DELICATE, FRILLED
RIB. YOU CAN, OF COURSE, ADD MILD, OR EVEN HOT, FRESH CHILI CUT INTO FINE SHREDS.

*3 ounces bean thread vermicelli (wun see)*

*¼ ounce dried white fungus (optional)*

*½ red bell pepper, seeded*

*½ green bell pepper, seeded*

*1 large red onion*

*1 cucumber, about 6 inches long, seeded*

*1 piece Japanese white radish, about 4
    inches long, peeled*

*1 small carrot, peeled*

*1 celery stalk*

*8 snow peas*

*1 small bunch watercress, (optional)*

*1 small bunch fresh coriander (cilantro)*

For the Dressing

*⅓ cup freshly squeezed lime or lemon juice*

*1 tablespoon fish sauce or light soy sauce*

*1 teaspoon* sambal ulek *or other chili
    paste*

*2½ tablespoons medium-light palm
    sugar or soft brown sugar*

*1 tablespoon finely minced lemongrass or
    grated lime or lemon zest*

*Tomato wedges, for garnish*

Soak the vermicelli and white fungus (if using) separately in hot water to cover for 15 minutes. Meanwhile, cut the bell peppers, onion, cucumber, radish, carrot, celery, and snow peas into matchstick strips. Remove the stems from the watercress (if using) and the coriander leaves. Combine all the salad ingredients in a bowl.

Drain the vermicelli and cut into 2-inch lengths. Drain the white fungus and chop into small pieces, discarding any woody parts. Place the vermicelli and fungus in another bowl. Add all the dressing ingredients to the vermicelli and fungus, and allow to marinate for 10 minutes.

Add the vermicelli, fungus, and dressing to the other vegetables, and mix well. Mound in the center of a serving dish. Surround with tomato wedges and serve.

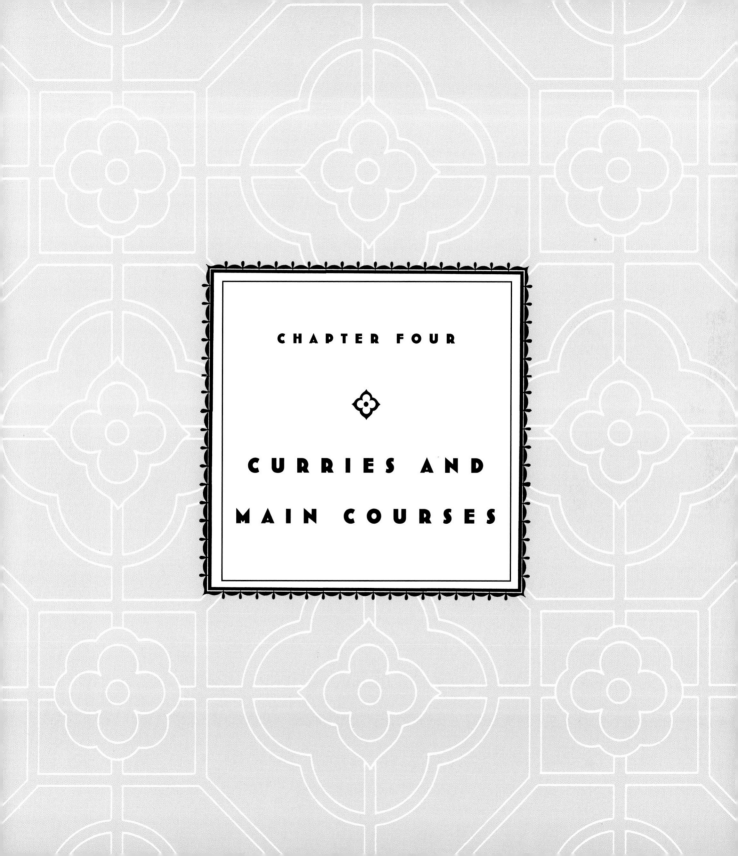

CHAPTER FOUR

CURRIES AND
MAIN COURSES

# CURRIES AND MAIN COURSES

CURRIES ARE THE MAINSTAY OF THAI CUISINE AND COME IN MANY VARIETIES. PERHAPS THE MOST WELL KNOWN ARE RED CURRIES, NAMED FOR THE POTENT CURRY PASTE USED TO FLAVOR AND COLOR THEM. Red chili, the roots, stems and leaves of fresh coriander, the citrus aromatics—kaffir lime leaves, zest, and juice and lemongrass—native ginger (galangal), and garlic are the fresh ingredients, ground together with pungent shrimp paste. Thai green curries are often deceptively hot, as they use green chilies and fresh-picked peppercorns. *Phanaeng* curries are aromatic, coconut-based dishes, their pungency moderated by the inclusion of ground roasted peanuts. Mussaman curries are on the milder end of the heat scale, their spicing influenced by Indian cuisine.

Curries are supplemented by small dishes smothered in potent chili-based sauces, and adaptations of stir-fried dishes introduced by migrants from southern China. In the nonvegetarian diet, grilled chicken and steamed, boiled, or grilled seafood further expand the range of main courses. It is usual, although not a requirement, to serve more than one main course, or at least one main course and a vegetable side dish at a meal, with a dish of rice and often noodles as well. In Thailand, main course dishes are placed in the center of the table, and diners eat from plates using a fork and spoon. No meal in Thailand is complete without rice, and a jar of hot chili sauce is usually present on the table.

# MUSSAMAN CURRY OF POTATO AND PUMPKIN WITH PEANUTS

SERVES 4 TO 6

Sᴇᴀꜱᴏɴᴇᴅ ᴡɪᴛʜ ɪɴᴅɪᴀɴ ꜱᴘɪᴄᴇꜱ ʀᴀᴛʜᴇʀ ᴛʜᴀɴ ᴛʀᴀᴅɪᴛɪᴏɴᴀʟ ᴛʜᴀɪ ᴄᴜʀʀʏ ᴘᴀꜱᴛᴇꜱ, **GAENG MUSSAMAN** ɪꜱ ᴏɴᴇ ᴏꜰ ᴛʜᴇ ᴅᴇʟɪɢʜᴛꜱ ᴏꜰ ᴛʜᴀɪ ᴄᴜɪꜱɪɴᴇ. ᴛʜɪꜱ ᴠᴇɢᴇᴛᴀʀɪᴀɴ ʀᴇᴄɪᴘᴇ ᴜꜱᴇꜱ ᴘᴏᴛᴀᴛᴏ ᴀɴᴅ ᴘᴜᴍᴘᴋɪɴ, ʙᴜᴛ ɪᴛ ᴄᴀɴ ʙᴇ ᴍᴀᴅᴇ ᴡɪᴛʜ ꜰɪʀᴍ ꜰʀᴇꜱʜ ᴏʀ ꜰʀɪᴇᴅ ᴛᴏꜰᴜ, ᴡʜᴇᴀᴛ ɢʟᴜᴛᴇɴ ᴏʀ ᴛᴇᴍᴘᴇʜ. ᴛʜᴇ ᴘᴇᴀɴᴜᴛ ʙᴜᴛᴛᴇʀ ᴄʀᴇᴀᴛᴇꜱ ᴀ ʀɪᴄʜᴇʀ ꜱᴀᴜᴄᴇ, ʙᴜᴛ ɪᴛ ᴄᴀɴ ʙᴇ ᴏᴍɪᴛᴛᴇᴅ.

Peel the potatoes and pumpkin and cut them into 1½-inch pieces. In a saucepan large enough to accommodate the vegetables, place ½ cup of the coconut cream and the curry paste. Place over medium heat and cook, stirring occasionally, for about 6 minutes until the coconut cream is well reduced and very aromatic. Add the potatoes and cook for 2 minutes, turning frequently. Then add the remaining coconut cream, the water, cardamom, cinnamon stick, bay leaves, and star anise or fennel seeds and bring to a boil. Reduce the heat to medium and simmer for about 8 minutes. Add the pumpkin, the onions or shallots, the nuts and the frozen spinach, if using. Continue to simmer until all of the vegetables are tender, about 14 minutes longer.

Stir in the fresh spinach leaves or pineapple, if using, and add the fish sauce or soy sauce, sugar, and tamarind or citrus juice. Check the seasoning, adding salt and pepper if needed. Stir in the peanut butter, if using, and cook over low heat for a few minutes. Transfer to a deep serving bowl and serve.

NOTES: One-half teaspoon fennel seeds may be substituted for the star anise. One-quarter cup of fish sauce may be substituted for the soy sauce for a more authentic flavor.

1½ pounds baking potatoes

1 piece pumpkin, 10 ounces

2 cups coconut cream

¼ cup Mussaman Curry Paste (page 15)

1 cup water

4 green cardamom pods

1 cinnamon stick, 2 inches long

2 bay leaves

1 point from a star anise (see notes)

14 small yellow onions, or 8 large shallots

⅓ cup unsalted roasted peanuts or pine nuts

1 small bunch spinach, stems removed; 2 ounces thawed frozen chopped spinach; or 1 cup cubed pineapple

1½ tablespoons light soy sauce (see notes)

2 teaspoons medium-light palm sugar or soft brown sugar

1½ teaspoons tamarind concentrate or 1 tablespoon lemon or lime juice

Salt and white pepper, to taste

1½ tablespoons peanut butter (optional)

# ROOT VEGETABLES IN RED CURRY

SERVES 4 TO 6

**I**F YOU PREFER A CURRY WITH PLENTY OF SAUCE, INCREASE THE WATER OR COCONUT CREAM TO GIVE YOU THE EXTRA VOLUME. ADDITIONAL COCONUT CREAM WILL MAKE THE CURRY MILDER IN HEAT AND MORE SUBTLE IN FLAVOR, SO ADJUST THE SEASONINGS TO SUIT.

2 to 3 tablespoons peanut or vegetable oil

1½ cups (8 ounces) chopped yellow
onion

2 large garlic cloves, sliced

½ to 1½ tablespoons Red Curry Paste
(page 14)

1¾ cups (8 to 9 ounces) peeled and
cubed red-skinned sweet potatoes,
yam, or taro (1-inch cubes)

2 cups (10 to 12 ounces) peeled and
cubed golden sweet potato (1-inch
cubes)

2¾ cups (14 ounces) peeled and cubed
baking potatoes (1-inch cubes)

1 lemongrass stalk, trimmed and halved
lengthwise

½ cup water

1¼ cups coconut cream

Salt and freshly ground black pepper, to
taste

2 tablespoons chopped fresh coriander
(cilantro), plus fresh coriander
(cilantro) or basil sprigs for garnish

In a large, heavy saucepan over medium heat, warm the oil. Add the onion and garlic, and cook, stirring frequently, for 3 minutes. Add the curry paste and cook briefly, stirring almost constantly.

Increase the heat to medium-high and add the cubed vegetables and lemongrass. Using a large wooden spoon, turn the vegetables until they are well coated with the curry paste and have browned slightly, about 4 minutes.

Pour in the water and half of the coconut cream. Cover and bring to a boil. Reduce the heat to medium-low and cook without disturbing for about 6 minutes. Stir once, add salt and pepper, and continue to cook until the vegetables are tender, about 6 minutes more.

Pour in the remaining coconut cream and heat gently. Stir in the chopped coriander and transfer to a deep serving dish. Garnish with the coriander or basil sprigs and serve.

# PHANAENG CURRY OF TOFU, MUSHROOMS, AND EGGPLANT

THE WORD **PHANAENG**, ALSO SPELLED **PANANG** OR **PENANG**, ON A THAI MENU USUALLY DESIGNATES A MILD CURRY-STYLE DISH BASED ON COCONUT CREAM THAT CONTAINS PEANUTS. RED CURRY PASTE (PAGE 14) CAN BE USED INSTEAD OF MUSSAMAN CURRY PASTE. IN THIS RECIPE I PREFER THE RESULTS WHEN I USE THE LATTER. IF YOUR TASTE IS FOR A HOTTER DISH, USE THE RED PASTE.

2 slender Asian eggplants, each 6 ounces, cut crosswise into 1-inch-thick pieces

Salt

1 tablespoon coriander seeds

1 teaspoon cumin seeds

1½ cups coconut cream

¼ cup Mussaman Curry Paste (page 15)

8 ounces firm tofu (bean curd)

1 cup peanut oil

½ cup unsalted roasted peanuts

12 large fresh oyster mushrooms, quartered, or 1 can (19 ounces) abalone mushrooms, drained

½ to 1 cup water

4 kaffir lime leaves, torn into strips, or 2 to 3 lime or lemon zest strips

1 to 3 mild fresh red chilies, halved lengthwise and seeded

2 tablespoons fish sauce, or 1 tablespoon light soy sauce

1 tablespoon medium-light palm sugar or soft brown sugar

Fresh basil leaves or finely shredded kaffir lime leaves

Place the eggplant in a colander and sprinkle generously with salt. Leave for 10 minutes, then rinse thoroughly and dry in a kitchen towel.

Heat a wok or large skillet without oil and dry-roast the coriander and cumin seeds, shaking the pan occasionally to turn them, until aromatic, about 2 minutes. Transfer to a spice grinder or mortar and grind or pound to a fine powder, then shake through a fine-mesh sieve to remove any large pieces. Wipe out the wok or skillet and set aside.

Pour ½ cup of the coconut cream into a saucepan and add the curry paste and ground spices. Cook over medium heat, stirring frequently, until the oil floats to the surface, about 6 minutes. Remove from the heat and keep warm.

Cut the tofu into cubes or strips. Heat the oil in the wok or skillet over high heat and fry the tofu until golden, about 2 minutes. Remove with a slotted spoon.

Still over high heat, add the eggplant pieces to the oil. Fry, turning and stirring them frequently, until golden brown and tender, about 3½ minutes. Retrieve with a slotted spoon and drain on paper towels. In the same oil fry the peanuts for a few seconds to crisp them. Retrieve with a slotted spoon. Add the tofu, peanuts, and eggplant to the saucepan along with the mushrooms, the remaining coconut cream, and enough of the water to cover the ingredients. Bring the sauce to a boil, reduce heat to medium-low, and simmer for about 5 minutes.

Add the lime leaves or zest, the chilies, fish sauce or soy sauce, sugar, and salt to taste, and simmer briefly. Transfer to a deep serving bowl and garnish with the basil or shredded lime leaves.

# GREEN VEGETABLE CHU CHEE CURRY

SERVES 4 TO 6

**T**HIS CURRY USES A HOT-LEMONY CURRY PASTE SIMILAR TO RED CURRY PASTE (PAGE 14) WHICH CAN BE SUBSTITUTED.

Cut the florets of broccoli from the stem, dividing them into bite-sized pieces. Using a small knife or vegetable peeler, peel the broccoli stem, then cut it on a diagonal, into ¼-inch-thick slices. Slice the celery in the same way.

Cut the chayote into bite-sized pieces. Remove the strings from the snow peas. Cut the bok choy in half lengthwise; if using spinach remove the stems. Steep the fried tofu in boiling water for 30 seconds, to remove surface oil. Drain. Cut the tofu or tempeh into ½-inch cubes.

To make the curry paste, combine all the ingredients in a mortar or spice grinder and pound or grind until a reasonably smooth paste is achieved.

Heat the oil in a wok or large saucepan over high heat and fry the tofu or tempeh until crisp and golden, about 2½ minutes for the tofu and 1 minute for the tempeh. Remove with a slotted spoon and set aside on a plate covered with paper towels to drain.

Pour off all but 1½ tablespoons of the oil and reheat the pan over high heat. Very, very finely slice the lemongrass and fry, stirring constantly, until crisp, about 1½ minutes. Add the curry paste and cook for 2½ minutes, again stirring constantly. Add the broccoli stems, celery, and melon or chayote. Cook for 1½ minutes, turning the vegetables frequently.

Add the scallions, snow peas, bok choy or spinach, and fried tofu or tempeh and mix well. Pour in the stock and add the fish sauce or soy sauce, sugar, and salt. Cook, turning the vegetables frequently, until they are all tender, about 8 minutes.

Pour in the coconut cream and heat for 1 to 2 minutes. Transfer to a serving dish and serve.

1 small head (6 ounces) broccoli

1 celery stalk

4½ ounces peeled and seeded chayote

6 large snow peas, about 2 ounces

6 very small bok choy, or 2 ounces
    spinach leaves

6 ounces fried tofu (bean curd) or tempeh

For the Curry Paste

3 large dried red chilies, seeded

2-inch piece lemongrass

¼ cup chopped shallots or yellow onion

1 cup peanut or vegetable oil

3-inch piece lemongrass stalk

1½ cups White Vegetable Stock (page 22)

2 tablespoons fish sauce, or 1½ table-
    spoons light soy sauce

1 teaspoon light palm or white sugar

Salt, to taste

½ cup coconut cream

6 large scallions

# TOFU CUTLETS ON STIR·FRIED GREENS

STICKS OF TOFU GRILLED WITH CURRY SPICES MAKE A SUBSTANTIAL MEAL OF STIR-FRIED CHINESE GREENS. EXTEND THIS ECONOMICAL MEAL WITH RICE OR NOODLES.

1 pound firm tofu (bean curd)

1 teaspoon Red Curry Paste (page 14)
    or mild curry powder

2 tablespoons peanut or vegetable oil

Salt and pepper, to taste

1½ to 2 tablespoons sesame oil

1½ pounds bok choy or other Chinese
    cabbage or greens, sliced

1 small fresh red chili, seeded and
    chopped, or 1 teaspoon sambal ulek
    or other chili paste (optional)

1 teaspoon minced or grated fresh ginger

2 tablespoons fish sauce, or 4 to 5 tea-
    spoons light soy sauce

½ cup White Vegetable Stock (page 22)
    or water

2 teaspoons cornstarch

1 cup (3 ounces) bean sprouts (optional)

Finely chopped fresh red chili or fresh
    coriander (cilantro)

Cut the tofu into 12 even-sized pieces. In a small bowl, make a paste of the curry paste or powder, 1 tablespoon of the peanut or vegetable oil, and a pinch each of salt and pepper. Brush the paste evenly over the tofu.

Preheat a heavy skillet or stove-top grill over medium heat. When hot, moisten with 2 teaspoons of the peanut or vegetable oil and 1 tablespoon of the sesame oil. Put the tofu in the pan or on the grill.

At the same time, place a wok or large skillet over high heat and add the remaining 1 teaspoon peanut or vegetable oil and 1 tablespoon sesame oil. When hot, add the bok choy or other greens, the chili or chili paste, and ginger and cook, stirring continuously, until the vegetables begin to soften, about 5 minutes.

While the vegetables are cooking, remember to turn the tofu from time to time so it is evenly browned. When done, after 3½ to 4 minutes, remove from the heat and keep warm while the vegetables finish cooking.

Add the fish sauce or soy sauce, salt, and pepper to the vegetables. In a bowl, mix together the stock or water and cornstarch and pour into the vegetable pan. Increase the heat, and keep stirring until the sauce thickens. At this stage, stir in the bean sprouts, if using, and cook just until they begin to wilt.

Transfer the vegetables to a platter or divide among individual plates. Place the tofu on top. Scatter a little chopped chili or coriander over the tofu and serve.

# VEGETABLE CURRY

SERVES 4

VEGETABLE CURRIES IN THAILAND INCLUDE NATIVE VEGETABLES SUCH AS THE SMALL ROUND GREEN EGGPLANTS CALLED **MAKHUA KHUN** AND THE STRANGE-LOOKING RELATIVE OF GINGER, **KRACHAI**, WHICH LOOKS LIKE A BUNCH OF BUFF-COLORED BABY CARROTS. IF THEY ARE OBTAINABLE, THEY CAN BE USED IN THIS DISH, KNOWN AS **GAENG PA JAY** IN THAILAND. YOU WOULD NEED ¼ CUP OF PEA EGGPLANTS AND ⅓ CUP OF SHREDDED **KRACHAI**, AND YOU WOULD ADD THEM WITH THE BEANS. IF YOU COOK THIS CURRY WITH A GENEROUS AMOUNT OF THIN SAUCE, IT'S BEST TO SERVE IT WITH COOKED BEAN THREAD VERMICELLI (**WUN SEN**) OR RICE VERMICELLI (**SEN MEE**). SERVE THE THICKER VERSION WITH STEAMED RICE.

Heat the oil in a medium-large saucepan over high heat. Add the curry paste and fry, stirring continuously, for 30 seconds. Pour in ½ cup of the stock and bring to a boil, stirring constantly. Simmer for 2 minutes.

Using ½ cup for a thick curry and 1½ cups for a thin curry, add the remaining stock and then the carrots. Bring back to a boil and cook for 2 minutes. Add the beans, zucchini, eggplant, chilies, and lime leaves or zest. When the cooking liquid has returned to a boil, reduce the heat to low, cover, and cook for about 10 minutes, stirring once or twice. Uncover the pan, add the corn, and continue to cook until the vegetables are tender, about 5 minutes longer.

Add the bean sprouts, sugar, and salt or soy sauce. In a small bowl, stir together the cornstarch and water, pour into the pan, and stir until the sauce becomes slightly thick and translucent, about 1½ minutes.

Stir in the basil or coriander leaves, reserving some for garnish. Transfer to a serving dish, scatter on the reserved herbs, and serve.

2 tablespoons peanut or vegetable oil

2 to 5 teaspoons *Red Curry Paste (page 14)*

1 to 2 cups *Dark Vegetable Stock (page 23)*

1 cup (4½ ounces) peeled and sliced carrots

1 cup (4 ounces) sliced long beans or green beans

1 cup (5 ounces) sliced zucchini

1 cup (4 ounces) sliced slender Asian eggplant

2 large, mild fresh red chilies, seeded and sliced

2 kaffir lime leaves, torn into strips, or 2 lime or lemon zest strips

6 ears canned or fresh miniature corn, halved lengthwise

1 cup (3 ounces) bean sprouts

1 teaspoon superfine white sugar

Salt or light soy sauce, to taste

2 to 5 teaspoons cornstarch

1 tablespoon water

½ cup loosely packed fresh basil or coriander (cilantro) leaves

# RED CURRY OF EGGPLANT AND PEAS

SERVES 4 TO 6

THAILAND'S VEGETABLE FARMERS LEAD THE WORLD IN THE VARIETY OF EGGPLANTS THEY GROW, FROM THE LARGE DEEP-PURPLE GLOBES WE KNOW IN THE WEST, TO THE TINIEST PEA-SIZED EGG-PLANTS THAT ADORN THEIR FIERCELY HOT "JUNGLE" CURRIES. THERE ARE WALNUT-SIZED EGGPLANTS TO EAT RAW WITH POTENT DIPS LIKE SALTY EGG RELISH (PAGE 39) AND GREEN CHILI DIP (PAGE 42), AND SLENDER LIGHT-SKINNED EGGPLANTS OF DELICATE FLAVOR TO ENJOY IN SALADS AND STIR-FRIES. ANY EGGPLANT, WHITE, GREEN, OR PURPLE, WILL DO FOR THIS CURRY. A HOT AND RICHLY FLAVORED DISH, IT IS AT ITS BEST PARTNERING STEAMED WHITE RICE AND A SIMPLE COMPANION DISH OF STIR-FRIED VEGETABLES.

*1½ pounds eggplants, cut into 1¼-inch cubes*

*Salt*

*1 cup peanut or vegetable oil*

*1 large yellow onion, chopped*

*1 tablespoon minced garlic*

*2 to 4 teaspoons Red Curry Paste (page 14)*

*1 cup coconut cream*

*½ cup (2½ ounces) sliced bamboo shoots*

*¾ cup (3 ounces) fresh or frozen green peas*

*1 cup Dark Vegetable Stock (page 23), or water*

*1 teaspoon tamarind concentrate or freshly squeezed lime or lemon juice*

*⅓ cup loosely packed fresh mint or basil leaves (optional)*

Place the eggplants in a colander and sprinkle generously with salt. Leave for 10 minutes, then rinse thoroughly under running cold water and set aside to dry, or dry in a kitchen towel.

Place a wok or large saucepan over high heat and add the oil. When hot, put in the eggplant cubes and brown lightly, about 3 minutes. Maintain a high heat during cooking, as this helps to prevent the eggplant cubes from absorbing the oil. Remove with a slotted spoon and drain on a rack over paper towels.

Pour off all but 2 tablespoons of the oil and add the onion and garlic to the pan. Cook on medium-high heat, stirring often, until well browned, about 3½ minutes. Add the curry paste and ½ cup of the coconut cream. Bring to a boil, reduce the heat marginally, and simmer until the coconut cream is reduced and there is a slick of red oil floating on its surface, about 7 minutes.

Return the eggplant to the pan and add the bamboo shoots, the fresh peas, if using, the remaining ½ cup coconut cream, and the stock or water. Cook gently for about 10 minutes, adding the frozen peas, if using, after the first 5 minutes of cooking.

Add the tamarind or citrus juice, with salt to taste and stir in the mint or basil leaves, reserving some for garnish. Transfer to a serving dish, scatter on the reserved herbs, and serve.

# CAULIFLOWER AND BEANS IN COCONUT AND PEANUT SAUCE

SERVES 4

M Y FAMILY ALWAYS ENJOY THE COMBINATION OF COCONUT CREAM AND PEANUTS IN A SAUCE. IT'S RICH, CREAMY, AND DELICIOUSLY NUTTY. WE DO THIS CURRY IN MANY VARIATIONS, USUALLY DEPENDING ON WHAT VEGETABLES WE HAVE ON HAND IN THE REFRIGERATOR. CHINESE (NAPA) CABBAGE OR THE FLESHY STEMS OF BOK CHOY OR SWISS CHARD, CUT INTO CHUNKS, CAN GO WITH GREEN PEAS OR EVEN SLICED ASPARAGUS IN THIS WONDERFUL, MILD CURRY SAUCE.

To make the sauce, place the onion, lemongrass, chili, ginger, and garlic in a blender, food processor or spice grinder. Grind to a paste, moistening with ½ cup of the coconut cream. When the ingredients are reasonably well ground, add the remaining coconut cream and the sugar and salt and process until as smooth as possible.

Pour the sauce into a saucepan and bring to a boil over high heat. Reduce the heat to medium-low and simmer for about 10 minutes. Add as much of the water as necessary to achieve the desired consistency, and then stir in the beans and cauliflower. Bring back to a boil, cover, reduce the heat to medium, and cook until the vegetables are tender, 8 to 10 minutes.

Add the fish sauce or soy sauce and peanut butter. Check the seasoning and adjust as needed. Cook until the peanut butter is thoroughly amalgamated with the sauce, stirring frequently. Transfer to a serving dish and serve.

NOTE: If you use the larger amount of water, you may need all of the peanut butter as well, or the sauce will be thin.

For the Sauce

1 small yellow onion, coarsely chopped

4-inch piece lemongrass stalk, chopped

1 mild fresh green chili, seeded

¾-inch piece fresh ginger

3 garlic cloves

1 cup coconut cream

1½ teaspoons light palm sugar or superfine white sugar

1 teaspoon salt

¾ to 1 cup water (see note)

2 cups (8 ounces) sliced long beans or green beans (1½-inch pieces)

2½ cups (9 ounces) cauliflower florets

1½ tablespoons fish sauce or light soy sauce

⅓ to ½ cup chunky peanut butter

# VEGETARIAN JUNGLE CURRY

SERVES 6

JUNGLE CURRY IS THE "GAME POT" OF NORTHERN THAILAND, AND ONE OF THE COUNTRY'S HOTTEST
AND MOST DISTINCTIVELY FLAVORED CURRIES. WHATEVER IS FISHED, PICKED, GATHERED, OR HUNT-
ED IS SIMMERED IN ONE POT WITH PLENTY OF CHILI AND SPRIGS OF GREEN PEPPERCORNS STRAIGHT
FROM THE PLANT. THIS VEGETARIAN VERSION REPLACES THE GAME MEATS WITH ROOT VEGETABLES AND
TOFU (BEAN CURD). SERVE IT WITH PLENTY OF PLAIN STEAMED WHITE RICE, OR WITH "STICKY" (GLUTI-
NOUS) RICE.

2 tablespoons peanut or vegetable oil

½ to 1 recipe Jungle Curry Paste (recipe
   follows)

1 bean curd stick or 1 sheet dried bean
   curd skin, soaked in cold water to
   cover for 10 minutes

6 ounces fried or firm tofu (bean curd),
   cut into ¾-inch cubes

½ cup (2½ ounces) sliced bamboo shoots

1 cup (5 ounces) peeled and cubed yam
   or sweet potato

1¼ cups (5 ounces) peeled and cubed
   Japanese white radish or eggplant

3 cups Dark Vegetable Stock (page 23)

½ cup (2 ounces) pea eggplants (see
   note) or green peas

1 cup (4 ounces) sliced long beans or
   green beans

8 to 12 small straw mushrooms

8 to 12 small cherry tomatoes

3 kaffir lime leaves, torn in half

2 fresh green peppercorn sprigs, or 1 tablespoon drained green peppercorns in brine

Heat the oil in a wok or large skillet over medium-high heat. Add the curry paste and fry, stirring continuously, until fragrant, about 2 minutes.

Drain the bean curd stick or bean curd skin and cut into bite-sized pieces. Steep the fried tofu in a small bowl of boiling water for 30 seconds, then drain and dry in a kitchen towel. Add to the curry paste the pieces of bean curd stick or skin, the fried or firm tofu, bamboo shoots, the yam or sweet potato, and the radish or eggplant. Cook over medium-high heat for 3 minutes, stirring the ingredients so they are evenly coated with the curry paste.

Add 2 cups of the stock, cover, and bring to a boil. Reduce the heat to medium-low and simmer until the vegetables are almost tender, about 10 minutes. Add the pea eggplants or peas, beans, mushrooms, tomatoes, lime leaves, peppercorns, and the remaining 1 cup stock. This curry has a generous amount of thin curry sauce. If you prefer a drier curry, use only as much of the remaining stock as desired. Season with salt and cook for about 5 minutes over medium heat. Stir in the basil leaves and the fish sauce or soy sauce, and add a squeeze of fresh lime or lemon juice. Transfer to a deep serving dish, and serve.

NOTE: Pea eggplants (makhua puang) are small, native Thai eggplants with a mild but tart taste. They grow on bushes in clusters, resemble tiny green tomatoes, and add interesting, tart flavor highlights to dips and curry sauces. If you cannot find them, substitute tomatillos for similar flavor, or sour bamboo shoots (sold in bottles in Asian specialty stores) as a unique alternative. Alternatively, substitute green peas for appearance, and add freshly squeezed lime or lemon juice or tamarind concentrate to achieve the required sharp, tart taste.

Salt, to taste

⅓ cup fresh basil leaves, preferably holy
    basil (bai krapao)

Fish sauce or light soy sauce, to taste

Freshly squeezed lime or lemon juice, to taste

5 red shallots or the outer layer of 1
    red onion

4 large garlic cloves

1 lemongrass stalk, chopped

1-inch piece fresh galangal or ginger,
    peeled

1 small bunch fresh coriander (cilantro),
    including roots and stems

1 tablespoon Crisp-Fried Shallots
    (page 24)

2 teaspoons grated kaffir lime zest, 4
    dried kaffir lime zest strips, or 2½
    teaspoons grated lime or lemon zest

1 teaspoon yellow bean sauce

12 fresh green bird's eye chilies, or 6 to 8
    small, hot fresh green Thai chilies

½ teaspoon salt

1 tablespoon peanut or vegetable oil
    (optional)

# JUNGLE CURRY PASTE

Combine all of the ingredients in a spice grinder, mortar, blender, or small food processor. Grind or pound the ingredients to a smooth paste, adding the oil or a little cold water, if needed, to assist in achieving the right consistency. This recipe makes enough for one hot curry or two mild ones. If you plan to use only half, moisten all of the curry paste with oil instead of water, and cook it for 5 minutes over medium-low heat, stirring constantly to prevent it sticking. Transfer the unused portion to a small glass jar, smooth the top, cover with oil to prevent oxidation, and store in the refrigerator for no more than 2 weeks.

# TOFU AND BEANS WITH RED CURRY PASTE

SERVES 4 TO 6

THIS DISH IS AS PALATE SEARING AS THE NONVEGETARIAN VERSION OF PORK AND GREEN BEANS IN A POTENT CHILI SAUCE, SO IT IS USUALLY SERVED AS AN ACCOMPANIMENT TO A MILDER CURRY, OR TO A NOODLE DISH. IF YOU PLAN TO SERVE IT ON ITS OWN, MAKE SURE THERE IS PLENTY OF STEAMED RICE AND SOME SALAD VEGETABLES TO COUNTER THE CHILI ASSAULT. TRY FRAGRANT JASMINE RICE, GARNISHED WITH ROASTED PEANUTS OR TOASTED SESAME SEEDS, AND A PLATE OF SLICED CUCUMBER AND TOMATO WEDGES.

Cut the tofu into ¾-inch cubes, rinse in boiling water, and dry on paper towels or a kitchen cloth. Heat the oil in a wok or skillet over medium-high heat. Add the tofu pieces and fry, turning them frequently, until golden on all surfaces, about 3½ minutes. Remove with a slotted spoon to paper towels to drain. Scoop out 1½ tablespoons of the oil and place in a saucepan. Save the remaining oil for another use.

Heat the oil in the saucepan over high heat. Add the tomatoes and fry until they begin to blacken at the edges, about 2½ minutes. Add the scallions and fry briefly, stirring and turning constantly.

Add the curry paste and fry, stirring continually, until fragrant, about 30 seconds. Pour in 1 cup of the coconut cream and bring to a boil. Reduce the heat to medium-low and simmer the sauce until it is quite thick, about 6 minutes.

Increase the heat again and add the water, tofu, beans, and sugar. Bring back to a boil, then reduce the heat to medium-low. Cover and cook for 6 to 8 minutes, in which time the tofu should absorb the flavors of the sauce. Pour in the remaining coconut cream and heat through. Check the seasoning, and add a squeeze of lime or lemon juice to enhance the flavors.

Transfer to a serving dish and garnish with the curled chili shreds and a few sprigs of herbs.

12 ounces fried tofu (bean curd)

1¾ cups peanut or vegetable oil

2 well-ripened Roma tomatoes, quartered lengthwise

4 scallions, white and some greens, cut on the diagonal into 1½-inch pieces

1½ to 2½ tablespoons Red Curry Paste (page 14)

1¼ cups coconut cream

½ cup water

2 cups (8 to 9 ounces) sliced long beans or green beans (2-inch pieces)

1 teaspoon superfine sugar

Freshly squeezed lime or lemon juice, to taste

For the Garnish

Curled chili shreds (page 25)

Fresh coriander (cilantro), mint or basil sprigs

# CLAY POT OF FRIED TOFU AND VEGETABLES IN BROWN SAUCE

SERVES 6

I CAN'T THINK OF ANY DISH MORE PLEASING ON A COLD NIGHT THAN THIS POT OF VEGETABLES AND TOFU IN ITS RICHLY FLAVORED SAUCE. THE SMALLER FRIED TOFU CUBES (ABOUT 1¼ INCHES) ARE BEST FOR THIS DISH, AS THEY DEVELOP A SILKY, DELIGHTFULLY CHEWY TEXTURE WHEN SLOWLY COOKED.

Place the fungus and mushrooms in a heatproof bowl. Pour 2 cups boiling water over them and soak for 10 minutes. Meanwhile, place the fried tofu cubes in another heatproof bowl, pour on boiling water to cover, soak for 2 minutes, then drain. Place the vermicelli in the same bowl and add boiling water to cover, soak for 1 minute, drain, and cut the noodles into 2-inch lengths. Set aside.

Heat the oil in a wok or skillet over high heat. Add the tofu cubes and fry, keeping them moving and turning in the oil, until golden brown, about 3½ minutes. Remove with a slotted spoon to paper towels to drain. Reserve the oil for another use.

Preheat an oven to 375 degrees F. Remove the mushrooms and fungus from their soaking water with a slotted spoon. If the mushrooms have stems, trim them off close to the caps and discard, then cut the larger caps in half or quarters. Trim off and discard any hard woody parts from the fungus, and chop it finely.

Strain the mushroom liquid through a fine-mesh sieve and set aside. Place the vermicelli, fried tofu cubes, mushrooms, fungus, cabbage, bamboo shoots, the piece or shreds of ginger, and the scallions in a clay pot or casserole. Add the stock, 1½ cups of the strained mushroom liquid, and half of the oyster sauce. Cover and place in the oven.

Cook for about 35 minutes. Stir the casserole and add the remaining oyster sauce and the fish or soy sauce and pepper. Cook for 15 minutes more to complete the cooking. The ingredients will be tender and the dish very aromatic.

If the pot can withstand direct heat, transfer it to the stove top over gentle heat. Stir the cornstarch into the remaining mushroom liquid (there should be about ½ cup), pour into the pot, and stir until the sauce thickens and becomes translucent. If the pot cannot be placed on the heat, pour in the cornstarch liquid and stir for 1 minute, then return to the oven for about 5 minutes, and stir again. Garnish with the scallion greens and serve directly from the pot.

½ ounce dried black (wood ear) fungus

8 dried black mushrooms

Boiling water, as needed

18 fried tofu (bean curd) cubes (see above)

2 ounces bean thread vermicelli (wun sen)

1 cup vegetable or peanut oil

10 ounces Chinese cabbage, cut into 1-inch-wide slices

½ cup (2½ ounces) sliced bamboo shoots

1-inch piece fresh young ginger or ½-inch piece mature ginger, peeled and finely sliced

6 scallions, including half the greens, cut into 1-inch pieces

1 cup Dark Vegetable Stock (page 23)

4 to 5 tablespoons vegetarian mushroom oyster sauce

1 tablespoon fish sauce or light soy sauce

Freshly ground black pepper, to taste

1 tablespoon cornstarch

Finely sliced scallion greens

# STIR·FRIED TEMPEH WITH GARLIC AND PEPPER

SERVES 4 TO 6

**Y**OU CAN EXPECT SEARING CHILI HEAT IN ANY THAI DISH WITH THE WORD **PRIK** IN ITS NAME. ADD TO THAT **GRATIAM,** MEANING "GARLIC," AND YOU HAVE A DISH THAT EPITOMIZES THAI CUISINE—HOT AND PUNGENT. **PAD GRATIAM PRIK THAI TEMPEH,** AS THIS DISH IS CALLED IN THAILAND, DELIVERS ALL THE FLAVOR ITS NAME PROMISES.

12 ounces tempeh or firm tofu
   (bean curd)

1 medium-large yellow onion

1½ tablespoons peanut or vegetable oil

1 tablespoon minced garlic

1 large, hot fresh green chili, seeded and
   sliced

1 red bell pepper, seeded and cut into
   matchstick pieces

4 ounces spinach or water spinach, stems
   removed

2 tablespoons vegetarian mushroom
   oyster sauce

1 tablespoon fish sauce or light soy sauce

½ cup water or White Vegetable Stock
   (page 22)

½ teaspoon white pepper

Salt, to taste

2 to 3 teaspoons toasted sesame seeds

Cut the tempeh or tofu into ¾-inch cubes. Cut off the top and bottom from the onion, then cut through the stem end, cut into narrow wedges and separate the layers.

Heat the oil in a wok or large skillet over high heat. When very hot, add the tempeh or tofu and the onion and stir-fry for about 3½ minutes. You will need to turn and stir constantly, but be careful you do not break up the tempeh too much. When ready, the onion will have softened and be slightly browned on the edges.

Add the garlic, chili, and bell pepper strips and continue to stir-fry over high heat for another 2 minutes. Add the spinach, the oyster sauce, and the fish sauce or soy sauce. Cook briefly, then pour in the water or stock and add the pepper and salt. Continue to cook over high heat until the green vegetable wilts, about 2 minutes.

Transfer to a serving dish, scatter on the sesame seeds, and serve.

# STIR·FRY OF WHEAT GLUTEN OR TOFU
# WITH STRAW MUSHROOMS

SERVES 4

WHEAT GLUTEN AND TOFU ARE IMPORTANT MAINSTAYS IN THE VEGETARIAN DIET OF PEOPLE IN SOUTHEAST ASIA. BOTH ARE SOLD IN MANY FORMS, SUITED TO THE DIFFERENT TEXTURES AND TASTES REQUIRED IN VEGETARIAN COOKING, AND THEY ARE OFTEN INTERCHANGEABLE IN RECIPES. SOME FORMS ARE INTENDED TO EMULATE MEAT, WHILE OTHERS MAKE NO PRETENSE OF BEING ANYTHING BUT HIGH-PROTEIN, VEGETABLE-BASED, MAN-MADE PRODUCTS. WHEAT GLUTEN SHOULD, OF COURSE, BE AVOIDED BY THOSE WITH A GLUTEN INTOLERANCE.

Immerse the gluten balls or tofu cubes briefly in boiling water to remove surface oil, drain very well, then cut them in half.

Heat the oil in a wok or large skillet over high heat. When very hot, add the gluten or tofu and fry, turning and stirring continuously, for 1 minute. Add the cabbage and scallions and stir-fry for 2 minutes. Add the mushrooms, bamboo shoots, bean sprouts, soy sauce, oyster sauce, sugar, salt, and pepper. Reduce the heat to medium-high and continue to cook, stirring, tossing, and turning the ingredients almost continuously, until the cabbage is tender, about 5 minutes.

In a bowl, mix together the stock and cornstarch. Increase the heat, pour the cornstarch mixture into the pan, and continue to stir until the sauce is smooth and translucent.

Check the seasoning and adjust as needed. Transfer to a shallow serving dish, garnish with coriander, and serve.

12 bite-sized wheat gluten balls or fried
  tofu (bean curd) cubes, about
  5 ounces total weight
Boiling water, as needed
2 tablespoons vegetable oil
1 cup (3 ounces) cut-up Chinese cabbage
  (1-inch squares)
4 scallions, white and some greens, cut
  into 1½-inch pieces
8 large straw mushrooms, halved
½ cup (2½ ounces) sliced bamboo
  shoots
½ cup (1½ ounces) bean sprouts
1 tablespoon dark soy sauce
2 tablespoons vegetarian mushroom
  oyster sauce
½ teaspoon superfine white sugar
Salt and white pepper, to taste
1¼ cups White Vegetable Stock
  (page 22)
1 tablespoon cornstarch
Fresh coriander (cilantro) sprigs

# STIR-FRIED TOFU WITH BELL PEPPERS AND ONION

SERVES 4

**I**N THAI CUISINE THERE ARE MANY CHINESE-INSPIRED STIR-FRY DISHES. THIS ONE INTEGRATES THE THAI FLAVORS OF LEMONGRASS AND CHILI. FIRM TOFU IS IDEAL FOR STIR-FRIES, RETAINING ITS FORM AND TEXTURE WITHOUT BREAKING UP. YOU COULD INTRODUCE BEAN SPROUTS, SNOW PEAS, OR SMALL FLORETS OF BROCCOLI INTO THIS COLORFUL MIX OF PEPPERS AND TOFU.

*10 ounces firm tofu (bean curd)*

*½ red bell pepper*

*½ green bell pepper, or ½ celery stalk*

*1 yellow onion*

*1½ tablespoons peanut or vegetable oil*

*1 teaspoon sesame oil*

*1 large, hot fresh red or green chili, seeded and sliced*

*1 teaspoon minced garlic*

*1 teaspoon minced or grated fresh ginger*

*2 teaspoons minced lemongrass*

*2 tablespoons fish sauce or light soy sauce*

*½ teaspoon superfine white sugar*

*Salt, to taste*

*Vegetarian mushroom oyster sauce (optional)*

*Fresh coriander (cilantro) sprigs*

Cut the tofu into thin slices, then stack the slices and cut them into narrow strips. Remove the seeds and stem from the bell peppers and cut into very narrow strips. If using celery, slice finely on the diagonal. Cut off the top and bottom from the onion. Cut through the stem end into narrow wedges and separate the layers.

In a wok or large skillet over high heat, heat the peanut or vegetable oil and the sesame oil. When very hot, add the peppers or celery and the onion wedges and stir-fry, constantly stirring, tossing and turning the ingredients, until partially softened, about 3 minutes. Add the chili, garlic, ginger, and lemongrass and stir-fry briefly. Add the tofu and maintain the high heat as you add the fish sauce or soy sauce, sugar, and salt. Stir and toss the ingredients carefully to mix, and cook for 1½ to 2 minutes longer.

Transfer to a serving plate. If using oyster sauce, pour it on in thin streams, then garnish with coriander sprigs.

# VEGETABLE CUSTARD STEAMED IN SMALL PUMPKINS

SERVES 4

THIS ELEGANT DISH IS A SAVORY INTERPRETATION OF THE FAMOUS COCONUT EGG CUSTARD DESSERT, **SONKAYA,** WHICH IS STEAMED IN A COCONUT SHELL OR A SMALL SWEET PUMPKIN. SERVE IT WITH A STIR-FRY OF VEGETABLES AND STEAMED JASMINE RICE AS A MAIN COURSE, OR SLICE INTO WEDGES AND PRESENT WITH A SMALL SALAD AS A FIRST COURSE.

*1 cup coconut cream*

*2 teaspoons Red Curry Paste (page 14)*

*4 small, squat pumpkins, each about 1 pound*

*⅓ cup (1½ ounces) very finely sliced long beans or green beans*

*⅓ cup (1½ ounces) frozen green peas, thawed*

*½ cup (2 ounces) diced zucchini*

*½ cup (2 ounces) small straw mushrooms, finely sliced*

*2 tablespoons finely sliced scallions, white and some of the greens*

*1 large, mild fresh red chili, seeded and minced (optional)*

*4 eggs, beaten*

*½ teaspoon minced fresh ginger*

*1 tablespoon fish sauce or light soy sauce*

*Salt and white pepper, to taste*

*1 fresh kaffir lime leaf (optional)*

In a small saucepan, combine the coconut cream and curry paste, bring to a boil over medium heat, then reduce the heat to medium-low and simmer for about 10 minutes, stirring frequently, until well reduced.

Meanwhile, using a sharp knife, slice off the top of each pumpkin and discard, or set aside to use as a lid. Using a small spoon, scoop out the seeds and internal fibers and discard them (or save the seeds and roast to eat as a snack).

In a bowl, combine the beans, peas, zucchini, mushrooms, scallions, chili, eggs, ginger, fish sauce or soy sauce, salt, and pepper. Beat until evenly mixed. Remove the reduced coconut cream from the heat, and set aside to cool.

Assemble a steamer large enough to accommodate the pumpkins. Pour water to a depth of at least 1½ inches into the base of the steamer. Bring to a boil, then reduce to a simmer.

If using the kaffir lime leaf, fold it in half lengthwise and cut away the hard central rib. Then cut the leaf into threadlike shreds. Stir half of the leaf shreds into the egg mixture and then add the cooled coconut cream. Stir the mixture well and divide evenly among the pumpkins.

Set the pumpkins on the steamer rack and cover the top of each pumpkin with a piece of parchment paper or aluminum foil. (Place their lids on top, if using.) Cover the steamer and cook until the pumpkins are tender and the custard is set, 35 to 45 minutes.

Turn off the heat and remove the pumpkins from the steamer. Discard the paper or foil (replace the lids, if using), and place the pumpkins on individual plates. Scatter on the remaining lime-leaf shreds, if using, and serve.

# TARO AND VEGETABLE FRITTER WITH COCONUT CURRY SAUCE

SERVES 4

I WANTED TO CALL THIS A FRITTATA, BUT AFTER SEEING A MENU ITEM CALLED JAPANESE ANTIPASTO, I WAS STRUCK BY THE ABSURDITY OF SOME CROSS-CULTURAL APPELLATIONS. SO IT IS AN EGG FRITTER, ALBEIT COOKED LIKE AN ITALIAN FRITTATA, AND IT IS CUT INTO GENEROUS WEDGES FOR SERVING. A NONSTICK SKILLET OR A CAST-IRON PAN WITH A WELL-POLISHED INTERIOR GIVES BEST RESULTS. IT IS SEASONED WITH A PURCHASED GREEN CURRY PASTE OR WITH MY RECIPE FOR MUSSAMAN CURRY PASTE (PAGE 15). ENJOY IT AS AN INFORMAL MEAL WITH PERHAPS A STIR-FRY OF VEGETABLES AND SOME PLAIN RICE OR NOODLES.

In a saucepan over medium heat, combine the coconut cream, garlic, and curry paste. Heat until it is almost boiling, then reduce the heat to medium-low and simmer for 2 to 3 minutes.

In a heavy nonstick skillet over medium heat, warm 1 tablespoon of the oil. Add the taro, bell pepper, corn, beans, celery, coriander, and chili and mix well. Cook for about 3 minutes, stirring often. Pour in the coconut cream mixture and continue to cook, stirring often, until the vegetables are half cooked and have absorbed most of the liquid, about 4 minutes.

In a bowl, beat the eggs until blended and season generously with salt and pepper. Increase the heat to medium-high, and pour the beaten egg evenly over the vegetables. Using a spatula, very lightly stir and turn the vegetables so the egg is evenly distributed throughout. Cook for about 30 seconds, then reduce the heat to medium, cover, and cook until the fritter is firm to the touch, about 6 minutes.

Uncover and cut the fritter in half or in quarters. Using a spatula, flip over carefully. Increase the heat to medium-high. Drizzle the remaining ½ to 1 tablespoons oil down the edges of the pan so that it runs beneath the outer edge of the fritter. After 1 minute, again reduce the heat to medium, re-cover, and continue to cook until the fritter is golden on the underside and the vegetables are cooked through, about 5 minutes. You may want to turn the fritter a second time, to cook it fully without burning.

¾ cup coconut cream

1 teaspoon minced garlic

1½ teaspoons green curry paste or Mussaman Curry Paste (page 15)

1½ to 2 tablespoons peanut or vegetable oil

12 ounces taro, peeled and coarsely grated

⅓ cup (2 ounces) diced red bell pepper

⅔ cup (3 ounces) corn kernels

⅔ cup (3 ounces) sliced long beans or green beans

¾ cup (3 ounces) sliced celery with leaves

1½ tablespoons chopped fresh coriander (cilantro)

1 small, hot fresh red chili, finely chopped (optional)

3 eggs

Salt and white pepper, to taste

For the Sauce

1⅓ cups coconut cream

1 to 3 teaspoons green curry paste or
    Mussaman Curry Paste (page 15)

1 tablespoon fish sauce, or 2 to 3
    teaspoons light soy sauce

1 teaspoon light palm sugar or superfine
    white sugar

Salt and white pepper, to taste

1½ teaspoons cornstarch

2 tablespoons water

1½ tablespoons finely chopped fresh
    coriander (cilantro) or basil

Freshly squeezed lime or lemon juice
    (optional)

While the fritter is cooking, make the curry sauce. In a small saucepan, combine the coconut cream and the curry paste. Bring almost to a boil over high heat, then reduce the heat to medium, and simmer until the coconut cream is partially reduced, about 6 minutes. Add the fish sauce or soy sauce, sugar, salt, and pepper. In a small bowl, stir the cornstarch into the water and stir into the sauce. Continue to cook, stirring slowly, until the sauce thickens to the consistency of cream, about 1½ minutes. Stir in the coriander or basil, and add, if you like, a generous squeeze of lime or lemon juice.

Lift wedges of fritter onto warmed individual plates, spoon on the sauce, and serve.

VARIATION: You can, of course, use any variety of vegetables. Keep the taro as your main ingredient, but add perhaps chopped cauliflower or broccoli, green peas, chopped spinach, and/or parboiled chopped carrot.

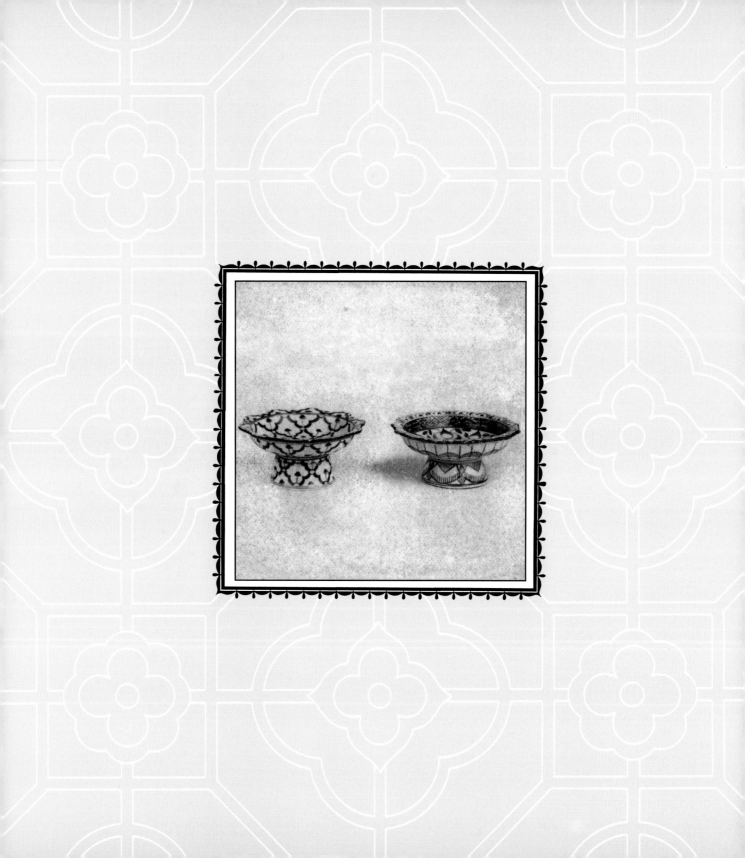

CHAPTER FIVE

VEGETABLE

SIDE DISHES

# VEGETABLE SIDE DISHES

**M**ANY OF THESE SPICY VEGETABLE SIDE DISHES WOULD MAKE A SIMPLE VEGETARIAN MEAL SERVED ON THEIR OWN, WITH RICE. In Thailand, they would accompany the main course or courses, selected to complement the dishes with which they are served. A crunchy, textural vegetable dish goes best with a smoothly sauced curry, for instance. Color is a consideration, too. The meal should be a rainbow of appealing hues, and the flavors of the side dish must enhance those of the main dishes. In Thai vegetarian communities, side dishes such as Crisp-Fried Spicy Vegetables (page 127) or Chinese Cabbage with Peanut Sauce (page 124) are served as a first course.

# SPICY STIR-FRIED CORN AND PEPPERS

SERVES 4

THE FRESH FLAVOR OF BASIL TRANSFORMS A SIMPLE BOWL OF CORN INTO A FRAGRANT ACCOMPANIMENT FOR NOODLES OR GRILLED OR DEEP-FRIED TOFU. I EVEN ENJOY THIS DISH WITH PLAIN ROASTED VEGETABLES. YOU CAN REPLACE THE BASIL WITH OTHER FRESH HERBS SUCH AS MINT OR CORIANDER (CILANTRO) AND MAKE THE DISH AS HOT AS YOU LIKE. IN THAILAND, I'VE EATEN A SIMILAR DISH THAT CONTAINED OVER 20 FIERCELY HOT BIRD'S EYE CHILIES.

Parboil the corn in lightly salted water for 3 minutes, then pour into a colander to drain.

In a wok or skillet over high heat, heat the oil. When very hot, add the scallions, garlic, bell pepper, and chili and stir-fry until the pepper has begun to soften, about 1½ minutes. Reduce the heat to medium-high, add the corn, and cook, stirring slowly, for 1 minute.

Add the fish sauce or soy sauce, salt, and sugar and mix well. Lightly stir in the basil leaves or other herbs. Transfer to a serving bowl and serve.

2½ cups (10 ounces) corn kernels

1½ tablespoons peanut or vegetable oil

2 scallions, white and some greens, finely sliced

1½ teaspoons minced garlic

1 small red bell pepper, seeded and cut into ⅓-inch squares

1 large, mild fresh red chili, seeded and chopped

1 tablespoon fish sauce, or 2 to 3 teaspoons light soy sauce

½ teaspoon salt

¼ to ½ teaspoon superfine white sugar, to taste

¼ cup small fresh basil, mint, or coriander (cilantro) leaves

# STIR·FRY OF MUSHROOMS WITH CHILI AND CORIANDER

SERVES 4

**Y**OU'LL FIND MANY TYPES OF CANNED AND DRIED MUSHROOMS IN ASIAN STORES. IN CANS ARE MOIST AND MEATY ABALONE MUSHROOMS, ELEGANT LITTLE GLOBE-SHAPED STRAW MUSHROOMS WITH THEIR INTRIGUING SOFT-CRUNCHY TEXTURE, AND DELICATE, SLENDER-STEMMED GOLDEN MUSHROOMS. IN THE DRIED RANGE ARE SHIITAKE MUSHROOMS, PRICED ACCORDING TO THEIR QUALITY, AND THE CRINKLY BLACK (WOOD EAR) AND WHITE FUNGI. I LOVE TO USE SEVERAL OF THEM TOGETHER IN A DISH, AND USUALLY COMBINE CANNED, DRIED, AND FRESH FOR THEIR DIFFERENT CHARACTERISTICS.

If only large straw mushrooms are available, cut them in half. Slice the abalone or oyster mushrooms, if large, and cut the smaller ones in half.

Combine the oils in a wok over high heat. When hot, add the mushrooms, scallions, garlic, and chili and stir-fry for about 1½ minutes. Add the soy sauce and sugar and cook, stirring frequently, until the vegetables are tender, about 1 minute.

Stir in the coriander and transfer to a serving dish. Garnish with the scallion greens, if using, and serve.

1 cup (7 ounces) small straw mushrooms

1 cup (8 ounces) canned abalone mushrooms, or 4 ounces fresh oyster mushrooms

2 tablespoons vegetable oil

1 teaspoon sesame oil

3 scallions, white and some greens, cut into 1-inch pieces

1 tablespoon minced garlic

1 large, mild fresh red chili, seeded and sliced (optional)

1 tablespoon light soy sauce

1 teaspoon superfine white sugar

½ cup loosely packed fresh coriander (cilantro) leaves

2 tablespoons finely sliced scallion greens (optional)

# BROCCOLI AND BEAN SPROUT STIR-FRY

SERVES 4 TO 6

JADE GREEN BROCCOLI COMBINED WITH CRUNCHY BEAN SPROUTS IS A HEALTHFUL VEGETABLE ACCOMPANIMENT TO ALMOST ANY THAI DISH. THE EGG THREADS ADDED AT THE END OF THE DISH CAN BE OMITTED, IF YOU PREFER.

2 small heads broccoli, 12 ounces total
    weight (see note)
1½ cups (4½ ounces) bean sprouts
½ cup water or White Vegetable Stock
    (page 22)
2 teaspoons cornstarch
2 small eggs (optional)
1 to 1½ tablespoons vegetable oil
½ teaspoon sesame oil
2 teaspoons light soy sauce
½ teaspoon superfine white sugar
Salt, to taste

Divide the broccoli into bite-sized florets. If using the stems, peel and slice them. Parboil the broccoli and stems in lightly salted water for just 1 minute, then drain in a colander and place under running cold water to cool.

You can give a touch of elegance to this dish by picking off the roots and seedpods from the bean sprouts. It only takes a few minutes to do, although it is not necessary to the success of the dish.

In a small bowl, mix together the water or stock and the cornstarch, and set aside. In another bowl, whisk the eggs, if using, until they are well broken up. Set aside as well.

In a wok or large skillet over medium-high heat, heat the vegetable and sesame oils. When hot, add the broccoli and stir-fry for 1 minute. Add the bean sprouts and stir-fry for 30 seconds longer. Add the soy sauce, sugar, and salt.

Stir up the cornstarch mixture and pour into the pan. Continue to cook over medium-high heat, stirring until the sauce thickens and becomes translucent. If you are not using the eggs, transfer the vegetables to a serving dish.

If you are using the eggs, remove the vegetables to a serving plate with tongs or a slotted spoon. Gently reheat the sauce over medium heat, then very slowly pour in the beaten egg in a fine stream so that it forms little threads in the sauce. Spoon over the vegetables and serve at once.

NOTE: I always select heads of broccoli that have firm, fleshy stems. They have a superb taste and texture not unlike asparagus, and if cooked crisp-tender are the appealing color of a ripe apple. Remove the tough skin from the stems with a vegetable peeler and slice them into elegant ovals, holding the knife at an angle diagonal to the stem.

# WATER SPINACH STIR-FRIED WITH GARLIC

SERVES 2 TO 4

**I**F THE HOLLOW-STEMMED WATER SPINACH, CALLED **PAK BUNG** IN THAILAND, IS NOT AVAILABLE WHERE YOU SHOP FOR ASIAN GREENS, USE FRESH YOUNG SPINACH INSTEAD. YOU CAN ALSO ACHIEVE GOOD RESULTS WITH FROZEN LEAF SPINACH. I LOOK FOR ANY EXCUSE TO ENJOY THE NUTRITIONAL BENEFITS OF TEMPEH. I DICE IT FINELY AND FRY IT UNTIL CRISP, AND THEN SCATTER IT OVER COOKED VEGETABLES. IT'S PARTICULARLY GOOD WITH SPINACH, SO IT IS WORTH PREPARING SOME WHEN YOU COOK THIS DISH.

Trim the thicker stems from the water spinach or regular spinach. Chop the water spinach into 5-inch pieces, leave regular spinach leaves whole. Place in a colander and pour boiling water evenly over the vegetable to wilt it, then leave to drain.

In a wok or large skillet over high heat, heat the oil. When hot, add the garlic and stir-fry until lightly golden, about 30 seconds. Add the fermented tofu and its brine, and break it up against the side of the pan. Add the water spinach or regular spinach and stir-fry over high heat until the leaves are glazed with the oil and well flavored with the garlic and tofu, about 1 minute. Add salt or, if you prefer, a splash of fish sauce. Transfer to a serving dish and serve at once.

*1 large bunch water spinach or regular*
*spinach, about 10 ounces, or 12*
*ounces frozen leaf spinach, thawed*
*Boiling water, as needed*
*1½ tablespoons vegetable oil*
*1 tablespoon minced garlic*
*1 teaspoon fermented tofu and its brine*
*Salt or fish sauce, to taste*

# CHINESE CABBAGE WITH PEANUT SAUCE

SERVES 4

**A**T HOME, I LOVE TO SERVE THIS AS A QUICK-AND-EASY FAMILY MEAL WITH A MOUND OF BITE-SIZED MORSELS OF FRIED TOFU OR TEMPEH ON TOP. IT ALSO MAKES A GOOD PARTNER TO CRISP-FRIED SPICY VEGETABLES (PAGE 127) AND PLAIN WHITE RICE.

½ to ¾ cup Peanut Sauce (page 20)

1 pound Chinese cabbage

2 tablespoons vegetable oil

½ cup White Vegetable Stock (page 22) or water

1 cup (3 ounces) bean sprouts

2 scallions, white parts only, cut on the diagonal into 1½-inch pieces

1 small, hot fresh red chili, seeded and sliced (optional)

Salt and white pepper, to taste

1½ tablespoons chopped unsalted roasted peanuts

Prepare the Peanut Sauce as directed, adding enough coconut cream and/or water to make a sauce of pouring consistency. Set aside.

Cut the Chinese cabbage leaves into 1-inch-wide slices, then cut the fleshy white base part of the leaves into ¼-inch-wide slices. This way the two will cook in about the same time.

Heat the oil in a wok or large skillet over medium-high heat. When hot, add the cabbage and stir-fry, turning and stirring almost constantly, about 2 minutes. Add the stock or water, raise the heat to high, and cover the pan. Cook for about 1 minute, then uncover the pan and add the bean sprouts, scallions, and the chili, if using. Continue to cook, uncovered and stirring and turning slowly and constantly, until the cabbage is tender and most of the liquid has evaporated, about 2½ minutes. Season to taste with salt and pepper.

Use tongs to transfer the vegetables to a warmed serving plate. Discard the liquid that remains in the pan. Spoon the peanut sauce evenly over the cabbage, garnish with the chopped peanuts, and serve.

# EGGPLANT IN YELLOW BEAN SAUCE

SERVES 4 TO 6

THE SALTINESS OF YELLOW BEAN SAUCE CONTRASTS BEAUTIFULLY WITH THE RICHNESS AND NATURAL SWEET FLAVORS OF EGGPLANT. THIS DISH NEEDS TO ACCOMPANY AN UNCOMPLICATED MAIN DISH SUCH AS TOFU CUTLETS ON STIR-FRIED GREENS (PAGE 98).

¼ cup peanut or vegetable oil

3 slender Asian eggplants, about 1
    pound total weight, unpeeled,
    cut into 1-inch pieces

1 tablespoon minced garlic

4 scallions, finely sliced, with white and
    green parts separated

2 tablespoons yellow bean sauce

2 teaspoons minced or grated fresh ginger

1 tablespoon light soy sauce

1 tablespoon superfine white sugar

¾ cup Dark Vegetable Stock (page 23)
    or water

Salt and freshly ground black pepper, to
    taste

Heat the oil in a wok or saucepan over high heat. When hot, add the eggplant and reduce the heat to medium-high. Cook, stirring frequently, until the eggplant is browned, 3 to 4 minutes. Add the garlic, white parts of scallions and some greens, and yellow bean sauce and cook, stirring, for 1 minute.

Reduce the heat to medium and add the ginger, soy sauce, sugar, and stock or water. Cook, stirring occasionally, until the eggplant is tender, about 8 minutes. Check for seasoning and add salt and pepper as needed. Transfer to a dish, garnish with the reserved scallion greens, and serve.

# CRISP·FRIED SPICY VEGETABLES

SERVES 4 TO 6

THESE VEGETABLES, FRIED IN A BRILLIANTLY CRISP, LIGHTLY SPICED BATTER, MAY BE SERVED AS A SIDE DISH WITH ANY CURRY MEAL OR EVEN WITH A BOWL OF NOODLES. **PAK CHUP PANG THOT**, AS IT IS KNOWN IN THAILAND, CAN ALSO BE OFFERED AS A FIRST COURSE, SNACK, OR HORS D'OEUVRE WITH SWEET CHILI SAUCE (PAGE 18) OR CHILI RELISH (PAGE 19), OR A SIMPLE DIP OF LIGHT SOY SAUCE AND CHOPPED GREEN CHILI. THE BATTER STAYS CRISP FOR SOME TIME, SO THERE IS NO SERIOUS URGENCY ABOUT GETTING THESE TO THE TABLE THE MOMENT THEY ARE COOKED. THEY ARE, HOWEVER, BEST EATEN HOT.

Peel the sweet potato and cut crosswise into 6 or 8 slices no more than ¼ inch thick. Cut the bell pepper in half and discard the stem and seeds, then, using a small, sharp knife, trim away the ribs. Cut the pepper 6 or 8 even-sized pieces. Cut the beans into 5-inch lengths; you should have 12 pieces.

Pour the oil in a wok or large, deep pan and set aside until the batter is made.

In a wide mixing bowl, combine all the batter ingredients, adding enough cold water to make a batter of creamy consistency that, when tested, thinly but evenly coats a piece of vegetable. Let stand for about 10 minutes, to allow time for the baking powder to activate.

Meanwhile, place the pan of oil over high heat. Line a large plate with several paper towels. When the oil is hot, reduce the temperature slightly. Working in batches of 8 to 10 pieces, one by one dip the vegetables into the batter and slip into the oil. Do not overload the pan. Fry until crisp, golden brown, and cooked through, about 2 minutes; the time will vary with the kind of vegetable being fried. Remove with a slotted spoon and drain well on the towel-lined plate. Repeat with the remaining vegetables and batter. Serve on a platter.

NOTE: Other vegetables can be cooked in this manner. Try scallions (white part and about 3 inches of green), yam or pumpkin (cut in the same way as sweet potato), ⅓-inch-thick slices of eggplant or zucchini, or baby carrots or miniature corn halved lengthwise.

1 golden sweet potato, 5 ounces

1 red bell pepper

3 ounces long or green beans

3 cups peanut or vegetable oil

For the Batter

½ cup all-purpose flour

⅓ cup rice flour

⅓ cup coconut cream

1½ teaspoons salt

1 to 2 teaspoons sambal ulek or other chili paste, or 1 to 2 teaspoons ground dried chili

½ teaspoon minced garlic

1 tablespoon very finely minced scallion greens or coriander (cilantro) leaves

½ teaspoon ground turmeric

½ teaspoon white pepper

1 teaspoon baking powder

# VEGETABLE STIR-FRY WITH CASHEW NUTS AND CHILI

SERVES 4 TO 6

**Y**OU CAN USE ANY COMBINATION OF VEGETABLES IN THIS DISH. BEGIN BY ADDING THOSE THAT TAKE LONGER TO COOK, AND THEN ADD THE QUICKER-COOKING ONES. THAT WAY, EVERYTHING IS READY AT THE SAME TIME. SUBSTITUTE BLANCHED ALMONDS, PINE NUTS, PECANS, OR WALNUT PIECES FOR THE CASHEWS, IF YOU LIKE. THAI COOKS PREFER TO WORK WITH RAW NUTS, FRYING THEM IN OIL TO ENHANCE THEIR RICH, NUTTY TASTE. YOU MAY PREFER TO USE READY-ROASTED NUTS, OR TO ROAST THEM IN AN OVEN OR MICROWAVE.

Heat the ¾ cup of oil in a small saucepan over high heat. When hot, add the cashews. Cook, stirring and shaking the pan almost continuously, until they are barely golden, about 2 minutes. Do not cook the nuts until they are brown, as they will continue to cook when removed from the oil. Retrieve with a slotted spoon and set aside on paper towels to drain.

Cut a slice off the top and bottom of the onion. Cut through the stem end into narrow wedges, then separate the layers.

Heat the 1½ tablespoons oil in a wok or skillet over high heat. Put in the onion, broccoli, carrot, and beans and stir-fry them for 2 minutes. Add ½ cup of the water and cover the pan. Allow the vegetables to steam-cook, stirring them occasionally, until almost crisp-tender, about 2½ minutes.

Remove the lid, and keeping the heat on high, add the zucchini, bamboo shoots, and corn and stir-fry for about 1½ minutes. Finally, add the bean sprouts, if using, and the ginger, chili paste, soy sauce, sugar, and salt, and stir together for a short time, until well mixed.

Stir the cornstarch into the remaining ½ cup water, and pour over the vegetables. Stir over high heat, until the sauce thickens, about 1½ minutes. Stir in the cashews, transfer to a serving dish, and serve at once.

NOTE: If using fresh miniature corn, parboil in lightly salted boiling water for 2 minutes, then drain before stir-frying.

¾ cup plus 1½ tablespoons vegetable oil

½ cup (3 ounces) raw cashew nuts

1 medium-large yellow onion

1 cup (4 ounces) broccoli florets

1 cup (5 ounces) peeled and finely sliced carrot

1 cup (5 ounces) sliced long beans or green beans

1 cup water

1 cup (5 ounces) sliced zucchini

½ cup (2½ ounces) sliced bamboo shoots

6 ears canned or fresh miniature corn (see note)

1 cup (3 ounces) bean sprouts (optional)

1 tablespoon very finely shredded fresh ginger

1 to 2 teaspoons sambal ulek or other chili paste

1 tablespoon light soy sauce

½ teaspoon superfine white sugar

½ teaspoon salt

1½ teaspoons cornstarch

# SAUTÉED PUMPKIN GARNISHED WITH CRISP GARLIC

SERVES 4

I FOUND I HAD THE BEST RESULTS COOKING THIS DISH IN A NONSTICK PAN. IT ALLOWED ME TO USE THE LEAST AMOUNT OF OIL AND NOT BE CONCERNED ABOUT THE PUMPKIN STICKING. ALTERNATIVELY, I TESTED IT IN MY FAVORITE CAST-IRON PAN, WHICH IS SO BEAUTIFULLY SEASONED FROM YEARS OF USE AND CARE THAT NOTHING EVER STICKS.

*1 small pumpkin, about 1½ pounds*

*1 tablespoon sesame oil*

*1 tablespoon vegetable oil (optional)*

*4 large garlic cloves, finely sliced*

*1¼ teaspoons minced or grated fresh ginger*

*1 teaspoon superfine white sugar*

*1 tablespoon light soy sauce*

*1 fresh kaffir lime leaf, very finely shredded (see note), or 1 tablespoon finely chopped fresh coriander (cilantro)*

*Salt, to taste*

*Lime or lemon wedges*

Quarter the pumpkin, scrape out the seeds and internal fibers, and peel. Cut into ⅓-inch-thick slices, then into pieces about 2½ inches long by 1 inch wide.

Heat the sesame oil, and the vegetable oil if using, in a nonstick pan over medium heat. Add the garlic and fry until golden brown. Remove with a slotted spoon and set aside on a paper towel to drain. Do not overcook the garlic, or it will become too bitter to use.

Add the pumpkin to the pan and cook, turning it carefully from time to time with tongs or a spatula, until beginning to soften, about 6 minutes. Add the ginger and cook 3 minutes more, again turning carefully from time to time. Season with the sugar and soy sauce. Cover, and cook over medium heat, turning occasionally, until the pumpkin is tender, about 5 minutes.

Scatter on the shredded lime leaf or coriander and the salt. Carefully transfer the tender pumpkin to a serving plate and garnish with the fried garlic. Serve with lime or lemon wedges.

NOTE: When kaffir lime leaves are finely shredded to use as a garnish, they should be fresh leaves, not dried or frozen. Fold a leaf in half lengthwise and cut away the tough central rib, then, using a small, sharp knife, cut across the leaf into fine, threadlike strips.

# TOFU AND TOMATO STIR·FRY

WHEN PORTUGUESE TRADERS BROUGHT CHILIES TO ASIA, THEY ALSO INTRODUCED TOMATOES, WHICH ARE NOW CULTIVATED EXTENSIVELY IN THAT REGION. WHILE TOMATOES MAY NEVER HAVE ASSUMED THE STAR STATUS OF CHILIES, THEY DO MAKE CAMEO APPEARANCES IN MANY THAI DISHES, LIKE THIS ONE.

Cut the tofu into thin slices, then cut into pieces 2 inches long by 1 inch wide. In a wok or skillet over high heat, warm the oil. When hot, add the tofu and fry, turning from time to time, until golden, 3 to 4 minutes. Remove with a slotted spoon to paper towels to drain. Pour off all but 1½ tablespoons of the oil from the pan.

Return the pan to high heat and add the scallions and garlic. Stir-fry for about 30 seconds, then add the sugar, chili paste, and soy sauce. Mix well, then return the tofu to the pan and add the water or stock. Bring to a boil, reduce the heat to medium, and simmer for 2 to 3 minutes.

Add the tomatoes, tamarind or citrus juice, salt, and pepper. Cover and simmer over medium heat, stirring occasionally, for about 5 minutes. Uncover and continue to cook, stirring occasionally, until the tomatoes have cooked down to coat the tofu, about 2½ minutes longer. Stir in the basil or coriander, transfer to a serving dish, and serve.

12 ounces firm tofu (bean curd)

½ cup vegetable oil

4 large scallions, cut into 1-inch pieces, white and some green parts

2 to 3 teaspoons minced garlic

1 tablespoon superfine white sugar

3 to 4 teaspoons sambal ulek or other chili paste

1 teaspoon light soy sauce

¾ cup water or White Vegetable Stock (page 22)

2 well-ripened tomatoes, cut into small wedges

2 teaspoons tamarind concentrate, or 1 tablespoon freshly squeezed lime or lemon juice

¼ to ½ teaspoon salt

½ teaspoon white pepper

½ cup loosely packed fresh basil or coriander (cilantro) leaves

CHAPTER SIX

◈

RICE AND

NOODLES

# RICE AND NOODLES

FRAGRANT, SLENDER JASMINE RICE COOKED PLAIN IS THE CONNOISSEUR'S CHOICE TO ACCOMPANY A CURRY OR SPICY DISH IN CENTRAL AND SOUTHERN THAILAND. In the north, however, steamed "sticky" (glutinous) rice is preferred with meals. Fried and flavored rice dishes are also more popular as snack foods, although may accompany a formal meal. Rice is served in a covered bowl, which is left at the table for diners to help themselves. Dining customs in Thailand dictate that the rice should never be flooded with sauce, so curries should be served beside the rice on a plate, and the diner can select both rice and main dish with each mouthful. Etiquette further demands that each main-course dish be eaten separately, even though they are all placed on the table together. So diners should help themselves to one curry or other main course, and eat that with rice, before sampling the next dish.

The best way to cook rice is by the absorption method, which involves placing the rice (washed and drained, or unwashed) in a heavy saucepan and adding water to a ratio of two parts rice to three parts water. The pan is covered tightly, the liquid brought to the boil, and then the heat is reduced to its lowest point and the rice is left to steam, that is, cook until it has absorbed all of the liquid and is dry and fluffy. This takes about 16 minutes. It can then be removed from the heat, but left in its closed pan for a further 5 to 10 minutes.

Noodles are considered more a snack food than a main menu item, although noodle dishes are often eaten as part of a meal. Rice sticks (*sen lek*) are the thin, flat, ribbonlike noodles used in stir-fried noodle dishes, while the gelatinous (*wun sen*) noodles are more suited to soups and salads. Egg noodles are also used in Thai cooking, usually in Chinese-style soups and stir-fries eaten as snacks. Fragile rice vermicelli, which fries to a crisp, snowy-white mass, is the base for the famous Thai sweet-sour noodles called *mee krob* (page 60), and is the starch component for endless varieties of simple soup-noodle dishes.

# THAI FRIED RICE WITH TOFU AND EGG

SERVES 4

THAIS PREFER THEIR FRIED RICE, HEAVILY SPICED WITH LOCALLY HARVESTED WHITE PEPPER. FOR THIS VEGETARIAN VERSION WITH TOFU, CALLED **KHAO PAD TAO HOO,** YOU CAN BE GENEROUS WITH PEPPER IF YOU ENJOY ITS ASSERTIVE TASTE. ADD PLENTY OF VEGETABLES, AS I HAVE DONE HERE, OR INCLUDE JUST ENOUGH FOR FLAVOR AND COLOR. LEAVING OUT THE EGG WILL NOT DIMINISH THE TASTE.

Place the rice in a heavy saucepan and add the water. Cover and bring to a rapid boil over high heat. Reduce the heat to the lowest setting so the rice cooks very gently (place a heat diffuser over the heat source, if necessary). Do not lift the lid for at least the first 10 minutes of cooking, then, if you want, stir the rice lightly with a fork and return the lid promptly. Cook until all the liquid has been absorbed and the rice is fluffy and dry, about 6 minutes more. Set aside.

In a wok or large, heavy pan over medium heat, warm 1 teaspoon of the peanut or vegetable oil. Rub the interior of the pan with a paper towel to smoothly and lightly oil the surface. Pour in the eggs, tilt the pan to spread the egg in a thin sheet, and cook until lightly golden on the underside, about 1 minute. Turn and cook the other side just long enough for the egg to set, about 30 seconds. Remove to a plate and set aside to cool.

Add another 1 tablespoon of the peanut or vegetable oil to the pan and increase the heat to high. Add the tofu and cook, stirring frequently, until golden brown and crisp, about 3 minutes. Remove with a slotted spoon to paper towels to drain.

Reheat the pan over high heat and add the remaining peanut or vegetable oil and the sesame oil. When the pan is very hot, add the garlic and fry for a few seconds. Add the white parts of the scallions and some of the greens, the mushrooms, corn, tomato, and bean sprouts and stir-fry over high heat for about 1½ minutes.

Add the cooked rice and soy sauce and cook, stirring, tossing, and turning the rice and vegetables until they are well mixed and heated through, about 2 minutes. Check the seasoning, and add salt and plenty of white pepper.

Roll the egg crêpe into a cylinder and cut crosswine into fine shreds. Finally, stir in half of the fried tofu and half of the egg, then transfer to a serving dish. Garnish with the remaining tofu and egg and the reserved scallion greens.

1½ cups long-grain white rice

2 cups water

2½ tablespoons peanut or vegetable oil

2 eggs, beaten

1 cup (5 ounces) firm tofu (bean curd)

2 teaspoons sesame oil

2 to 3 teaspoons crushed or finely minced garlic

⅓ cup sliced scallions, with white and green parts separated

½ cup (3½ ounces) sliced straw mushrooms or button mushrooms

½ cup (2 ounces) cooked corn kernels or chopped canned miniature corn

1 small tomato, seeded and diced

¼ cup (¾ ounce) chopped bean sprouts

1 tablespoon light soy sauce

Salt and white pepper, to taste

1 tablespoon crushed unsalted roasted peanuts (optional)

# PINEAPPLE FRIED RICE

SERVES 4 TO 6

SERVING RICE IN A PINEAPPLE SHELL IS A CHARMING TRADITION THAT BRINGS A FESTIVE ATMOS-PHERE TO THE SIMPLEST MEAL, EVEN A BARBECUE. IF YOU PREFER, SERVE IT IN A MEDIUM-SIZED SERVING DISH, MOUNDING IT HIGH, AS THEY DO IN THAILAND. ALTHOUGH JASMINE IS THE PRIZED RICE IN THAILAND, I BELIEVE ITS DELICATE FLAVOR IS LOST WHEN COOKED IN A DISH LIKE THIS, SO REGULAR LONG-GRAIN WHITE RICE WILL DO.

*1 large, ripe pineapple*

*1¾ cups long-grain white rice*

*2½ cups water*

*2 tablespoons shredded coconut, toasted, for garnish (optional)*

*⅓ cup (1½ ounces) finely sliced long beans or green beans*

*2½ tablespoons peanut or vegetable oil*

*2½ teaspoons finely minced garlic*

*½ cup (2½ ounces) finely diced yellow onion*

*½ cup (2½ ounces) diced firm tofu (bean curd) or tempeh*

*2 teaspoons grated or finely minced fresh ginger*

*⅓ cup (2½ ounces) sliced canned straw mushrooms, or 2 ounces fresh oyster mushrooms, sliced if large*

*¼ red bell pepper, diced*

*1 mild fresh red chili, seeded and chopped*

*2 teaspoons tomato paste*

*1½ teaspoons mashed yellow bean sauce or fermented tofu and its brine*

*Superfine white sugar, to taste*

*Light soy sauce, to taste*

Cut the pineapple in half lengthwise, cutting straight through the crown (leaves). Using a sharp knife, remove the flesh from the skins. Cut the flesh into ½-inch cubes. You will need 1½ cups for this recipe. Turn the 2 empty pineapple skins upside down on a tray to drain.

Place the rice into a heavy saucepan and add the water. Cover and bring to a rapid boil over high heat. Reduce the heat to the lowest setting so the rice cooks very gently (place a heat diffuser over the heat source, if necessary). Do not lift the lid for at least the first 10 minutes of cooking; then, if you want, stir the rice lightly with a fork and return the lid promptly. Cook until all the liquid has been absorbed and the rice is fluffy and dry, about 6 minutes longer.

Meanwhile, in a small skillet without oil, toast the coconut if using, until golden, stirring constantly, about 2 minutes. Set aside to cool.

Parboil the beans in a small saucepan of lightly salted water for 1½ minutes. Drain and set aside. Heat the oil in a wok or large skillet over high heat. Add the garlic and fry, stirring constantly, for 30 seconds. Add the onion and diced tofu or tempeh, and stir-fry until lightly golden, about 3½ minutes. Add the ginger, beans, mushrooms, bell pepper, chili, tomato paste, and yellow bean sauce or fermented tofu. Stir over high heat for about 2 minutes, then add the rice and continue stirring, tossing, and turning until well mixed.

Stir the 1½ cups diced pineapple into the rice, and add the sugar and soy sauce. Cook a little longer until heated through. Mound the rice in the pineapple shells and garnish with the toasted coconut. Serve at once.

# COCONUT RICE

SERVES 4

**A**FTER TASTING THIS DISH, YOU MAY NEVER WANT TO EAT PLAIN RICE AGAIN. COCONUT RICE HAS A SLIGHT SWEETNESS AND SUPERBLY NUTTY FLAVOR, MAKING IT A PERFECT COMPANION FOR HOT CURRIES. TRY IT WITH VEGETABLE CUSTARD STEAMED IN SMALL PUMPKINS (PAGE 112).

*1½ cups long-grain white rice*

*½ cup shredded dried coconut*

*½ cup coconut cream*

*1¾ cups water*

*1½ teaspoons salt*

*1 small, hot fresh red chili, seeded and finely sliced*

*1 kaffir lime leaf, finely shredded (optional)*

Put the rice, coconut, coconut cream, water, salt, and chili in a heavy saucepan. Cover and bring to a rapid boil over high heat. Reduce the heat to the lowest setting so the rice cooks very gently (place a heat diffuser over the heat source, if necessary) without lifting the lid, for about 7 minutes.

Open the pan, add the shredded lime leaf, if using, and stir up the rice. Re-cover the pan and continue to cook until all of the liquid is absorbed and the rice is dry and fluffy, about 10 minutes longer. Remove from the heat and let sit, covered, for at least 5 minutes or for up to 15 minutes, before serving.

VARIATION: To make a festive golden coconut rice, add ¾ teaspoon ground turmeric at the start of cooking. Omit the lime leaf, and instead stir in 1 tablespoon chopped fresh coriander (cilantro) or a few fresh basil leaves just before serving.

# STIR·FRIED RICE STICK NOODLES WITH TOFU, PEPPERS AND EGG IN SOY SAUCE

SERVES 4

RICE STICK NOODLES PROVIDE A LIGHT, BUT SUBSTANTIAL MEAL, ESPECIALLY WHEN SUPPLEMENTED, AS IN THIS RECIPE, WITH TOFU AND EGG. YOU CAN, OF COURSE, OMIT THE EGG, OR REPLACE IT WITH AN ADDITIONAL VEGETABLE SUCH AS SMALL STRAW MUSHROOMS.

Place the noodles in a bowl, add hot water to cover, and let stand for 6 to 8 minutes to soften, then pour into a colander to drain.

If using the eggs, in a wok or skillet over medium-high heat, warm the sesame oil. Meanwhile, in a bowl, beat the eggs and season with salt and pepper. Pour into the pan and cook until set softly like an omelet. Fold in half and continue to cook until softly cooked throughout, turning once again if necessary to cook evenly. Remove from the pan and set aside to cool.

Pour the vegetable oil into the same pan and place over medium-high heat. Add the tofu strips, and cook, stirring and turning frequently, for 1½ minutes. Add the bell peppers and garlic and cook, stirring, until the peppers have softened, about 1½ minutes longer.

Add the drained noodles and stir over medium-high heat until well mixed and heated through. Add the soy sauce, sugar, salt, pepper, and the chili paste or chili oil and raise the heat to high. Continue to cook, stirring, for 1 to 1½ minutes, or until the seasonings are evenly distributed.

Chop the egg into ½-inch pieces. Add to the noodles, and toss to mix evenly. Transfer to a platter and garnish with the coriander or scallion greens and the chili shreds. Serve at once.

8 to 10 ounces rice stick noodles (sen lek)

1½ teaspoons sesame oil

3 eggs (optional)

Salt and white pepper, to taste

1½ tablespoons peanut or vegetable oil

4 ounces fried tofu (bean curd), cut into fine strips

½ red bell pepper, seeded, cut into matchsticks

½ green bell pepper, seeded, cut into matchsticks

1 teaspoon minced garlic

3 to 4 tablespoons light soy sauce

½ teaspoon superfine white sugar

½ to 1 teaspoon sambal ulek or other chili paste or chili oil

1½ tablespoons chopped fresh coriander (cilantro) or sliced scallion greens

Finely shredded fresh red chili

# GLUTINOUS RICE WITH PEANUTS AND MUSHROOMS

SERVES 4 TO 6

GLUTINOUS RICE IS A GREAT FAVORITE IN MANY PARTS OF SOUTHEAST ASIA, WHERE IT IS USUALLY REFERRED TO AS "STICKY" RICE. THE NAME COMES FROM ITS PLEASANT STICKINESS AND NOT ITS GLUTEN CONTENT, SO THOSE WITH A GLUTEN INTOLERANCE NEED NOT AVOID THIS DELICIOUS GRAIN. IN MOST PARTS OF NORTHERN THAILAND, "STICKY" RICE IS PREFERRED OVER REGULAR RICE AT MEAL-TIME. IT IS STEAMED SLOWLY, IN BASKETS, AND WHEN COOKED BECOMES SLIGHTLY TRANSLUCENT. IDEALLY THE RICE SHOULD BE SOAKED OVERNIGHT, TO FACILITATE QUICK COOKING. BUT IF YOU HAVEN'T THOUGHT AHEAD, SIMPLY COOK IT LONGER THAN REGULAR RICE, 30 TO 40 MINUTES.

Pour the soaked rice into a colander to drain. Meanwhile, in a wok or small skillet over high heat, heat the oil. When hot, add the peanuts and fry briefly until golden and aromatic. Retrieve with a slotted spoon and set aside on a plate.

Return the pan to high heat. Add the tofu, gluten, or tempeh and stir-fry for 2 minutes. Add the straw mushrooms and white parts of the scallion and stir-fry for 2 minutes. Add the rice, salt, pepper, soy sauce, and most of the scallion greens, reserving a little for garnish. Mix well and add the peanuts and bok choy.

Transfer the rice to a wide, shallow heatproof dish that will fit inside your steamer. Fill the steamer pan with water to a depth of 2 inches, bring to a boil, and then reduce the heat so the water is simmering gently. Put the dish of rice on the steamer rack, cover the dish with a piece of parchment paper or aluminum foil, cover the steamer, and cook until the rice is tender, about 25 minutes. Add hot water as needed to maintain the original level in the steamer pot. You may want to stir up the rice occasionally, to make sure it is cooking evenly.

Remove the dish from the steamer and serve the rice directly from the dish. Or press lightly into small bowls (a Chinese rice bowl is ideal) and invert the molds of rice onto individual plates, scattering on the remaining scallion greens.

2½ cups long-grain white glutinous rice, soaked overnight in cold water to cover

2 tablespoons peanut or vegetable oil

¾ cup (4 ounces) unsalted roasted peanuts

¾ cup (3½ ounces) diced fried tofu (bean curd), firm tofu, wheat gluten, or tempeh (¼-inch dice)

½ cup (3½ ounces) sliced canned straw mushrooms

2 scallions, sliced, white and green parts separated

1½ teaspoons salt

½ teaspoon white pepper

1 tablespoon light soy sauce

2 small bok choy, quartered lengthwise

# BEAN THREAD VERMICELLI BRAISED WITH SHIITAKE MUSHROOMS

SERVES 4 TO 6

A SIMPLE VEGETABLE DISH, SUCH AS VEGETABLE STIR-FRY WITH CASHEW NUTS AND CHILI (PAGE 129), GOES WELL WITH THE ROBUST FLAVOR OF THESE NOODLES. BOTH THE SHIITAKE MUSHROOMS AND THE **WUN SEN** NOODLES COMPLEMENT CHILIES, SO THIS IS AN OPPORTUNITY TO COOK UP SOMETHING REALLY HOT, IF YOU LIKE YOUR FOOD THAT WAY. EITHER INCREASE THE NUMBER OF FRESH CHILIES, OR STIR IN A TEASPOON OF **SAMBAL ULEK** OR CHILI BEAN PASTE.

18 dried or fresh shiitake (Japanese black) mushrooms

2 cups hot water

3 ounces bean thread vermicelli (wun sen)

3 scallions, white and some greens, cut into 1-inch lengths

½ cup (2½ ounces) sliced bamboo shoots

½ cup (2½ ounces) peeled and sliced carrot

1½ tablespoons dark soy sauce

1½ tablespoons light soy sauce

1 small, hot fresh red chili, seeded and finely sliced

1 teaspoon superfine white sugar

2 teaspoons cornstarch

¾ cup cold water

1 small bunch fresh coriander (cilantro)

Salt and white pepper, to taste

If using dried mushrooms, place in a bowl, add the hot water, and let stand for 25 minutes. Place the bean thread vermicelli in a separate bowl, add hot water to cover, and let stand for 10 minutes.

Remove the mushrooms from the water, squeezing out excess moisture. Trim the tough stems from the mushrooms, cutting off close to the caps. Strain the water through a fine-mesh sieve into a saucepan.

Drain the noodles in a colander and let stand for a few minutes. Add to the saucepan, along with the drained or fresh mushrooms, scallions, bamboo shoots, carrot, dark and light soy sauce, chili, and sugar. Bring to a boil over high heat, then reduce the heat to medium and simmer until the carrots are tender, about 8 minutes.

In a small bowl, mix together the cornstarch and cold water. Pour into the pan. Raise the heat and cook, stirring, until the sauce thickens and becomes translucent, about 2½ minutes.

Break off the tough stems from the coriander bunch and add the sprigs to the dish, stirring them in lightly. Check the seasoning and add salt and pepper. Transfer to a serving dish and serve.

# EGG NOODLES WITH CABBAGE IN VEGETARIAN MUSHROOM OYSTER SAUCE

SERVES 4

I'VE EATEN A DISH WITH THIS SAME COMBINATION OF VEGETABLES—CABBAGE, SCALLIONS AND MUSH-ROOMS—PREPARED WITH FRESH WHEAT-FLOUR NOODLES HANDMADE BY A CHINESE NOODLE-MAKING ARTISAN. HE BEGAN WITH A BALL OF MOIST FLOUR AND WATER DOUGH, WHICH HAD BEEN SOFTENED BY KNEADING FOR 10 MINUTES, AND THEN LEFT TO STAND FOR A FURTHER 10 MINUTES WHILE THE GLUTEN EXPANDED AND BECAME HIGHLY ELASTICIZED. IN JUST 4 MINUTES, WITH A SERIES OF DEFT STRETCH-INGS, FOLDINGS, AND TWISTS, HE HAD PULLED THE DOUGH INTO A MASS OF FINE, WHITE, SOFT NOO-DLES. THEY COOKED IN JUST 3 MINUTES IN SALTED WATER, AND THEN HE TOSSED THEM INTO THE WOK WITH THE VEGETABLES AND OYSTER SAUCE FOR A QUICK STIR-FRY. HEAVEN IN A BOWL! YOU CAN USE OTHER KINDS OF WHEAT-FLOUR NOODLES IN THIS DISH.

Bring a pan of lightly salted water to a boil, add the noodles, and cook until just tender, about 4 minutes. Pour into a colander to drain and set aside.

Heat 2 tablespoons of the oil in a wok or large skillet over high heat. Add the noodles and stir-fry until the noodles are glazed with the oil, about 1½ minutes. Transfer to a bowl and set aside.

Add the remaining 1 tablespoon oil to the pan and return to medium-high heat. Add the cabbage, scallions, mushrooms, and ginger and stir-fry until the cabbage has begun to soften, about 2½ minutes.

Stir together the stock and cornstarch in a small bowl. Raise the heat. Return the noodles to the pan and add the 4 to 5 tablespoons mushroom oyster sauce and the cornstarch-stock mixture, stirring well. Add the salt and pepper and cook, stirring and tossing the noodles until they are glazed with the sauce and the cabbage is tender, about 2 minutes.

Transfer to a serving plate and and garnish with extra oyster sauce and the sliced scallion greens.

*8 ounces dried fine egg noodles*

*3 tablespoons peanut or vegetable oil*

*2 cups (6 ounces) chopped Chinese cabbage*

*3 scallions, white and some greens, cut into 1-inch pieces, plus extra finely sliced scallion greens for garnish*

*½ cup (3½ ounces) sliced straw mush-rooms*

*1 tablespoon finely shredded fresh ginger*

*2½ cups White Vegetable Stock (page 22)*

*2 teaspoons cornstarch*

*4 to 5 tablespoons vegetarian mushroom oyster sauce, plus extra for serving*

*Salt and white pepper, to taste*

# VEGETARIAN PAD THAI NOODLES

SERVES 4

T HAI NOODLES ARE A DELICIOUS ONE-PLATE MEAL, SO I HAVE GIVEN A GENEROUS RECIPE FOR FOUR, WHICH WOULD SERVE MORE IF IT'S TO ACCOMPANY OTHER DISHES.

12 ounces rice stick noodles (sen lek)

8 ounces firm tofu (bean curd)

⅓ cup peanut oil or vegetable oil

1 cup (4 ounces) sliced celery

3-inch piece large carrot, cut into matchsticks

2 teaspoons minced garlic

2 teaspoons tamarind concentrate, or 1
   tablespoon freshly squeezed lemon
   juice

2 tablespoons light soy sauce

1 to 1½ tablespoons medium-light palm
   sugar or soft brown sugar

1½ teaspoons fermented tofu, mashed
   with its brine

¾ teaspoon sambal ulek or other chili
   paste

1 teaspoon sesame oil (optional)

Salt and white pepper, to taste

3 scallions, white and green parts,
   chopped

1¼ cups (4 ounces) bean sprouts

½ cup (2½ ounces) roasted unsalted
   peanuts, coarsely chopped

Chopped fresh coriander (cilantro) or
   sliced scallion greens

Place the noodles in a bowl, add hot water to cover, and let stand for 6 to 8 minutes to soften, then pour into a colander to drain. Cut the firm tofu into ½-inch cubes. Heat the oil in a wok or large skillet over high heat. Add the tofu cubes and fry, turning frequently, until crisp and golden, about 3 minutes. Remove with a slotted spoon and set aside on paper towels. Pour off all but 2 tablespoons of the oil from the pan.

Place the same pan over high heat. Add the celery and the carrots and cook, stirring often, until softened, about 2½ minutes. Add the garlic, fried tofu, and the well-drained noodles and stir over high heat until each strand of noodle is moistened with the oil, about 1½ minutes.

In a small bowl, combine the tamarind concentrate or lemon juice, soy sauce, sugar (to taste), fermented tofu, and chili paste. Pour over the noodles and add the sesame oil, if using. Continue to stir over high heat, tossing, lifting, and turning the noodles until evenly seasoned.

Check the seasoning and adjust to taste, plus add salt and a generous sprinkle of pepper. Add the scallions and bean sprouts, mix in well, and allow them to cook for about 45 seconds.

Lastly, stir in the peanuts, then transfer to a serving dish, or 4 large shallow bowls. Garnish with the coriander or scallion greens.

NOTE: Most rice stick noodles come in packs weighing about 14 ounces. Use the whole pack, if you prefer, adjusting the seasonings to taste. Leftover *pad Thai* reheats well in a microwave oven.

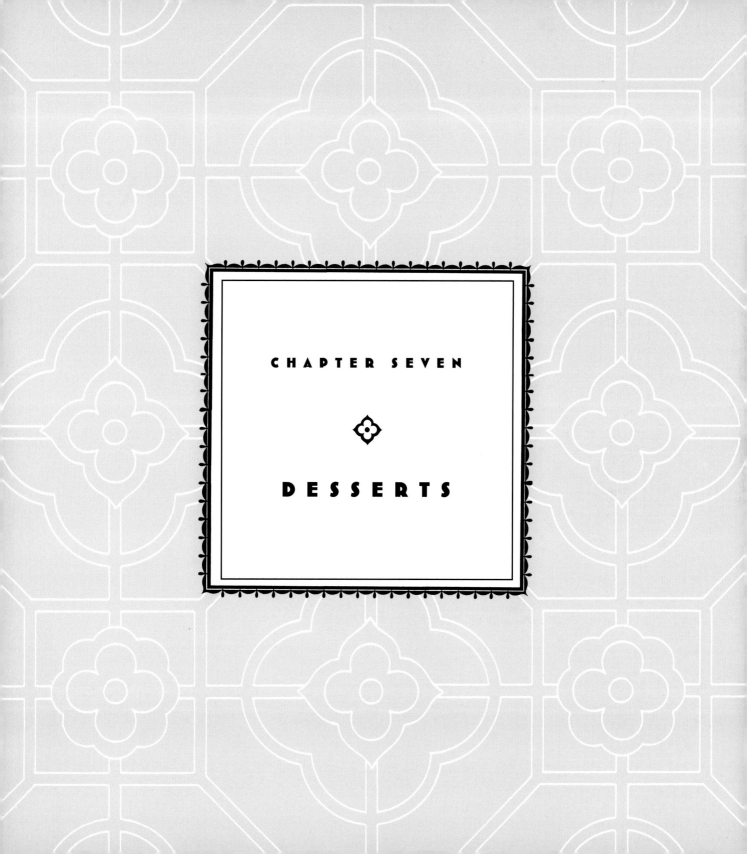

# CHAPTER SEVEN

# DESSERTS

# DESSERTS

**T**HAIS DON'T WAIT FOR MEALTIMES TO ENJOY THE SWEET SNACKS THAT ABOUND IN SHOPS AND STREET-MARKET FOOD STALLS ALL OVER THE COUNTRY. Nowhere else in Asia are desserts more important than in Thailand, which prides itself on the variety and invention of its desserts.

Coconut, rice, and bananas are foremost in the list of ingredients used in Thai sweets, and they are cooked together in a bewildering variety of ways: bite-sized morsels of sweetened rice batter steamed with coconut cream in small banana-leaf containers, fried bananas coated with coconut, bananas poached in coconut milk, rice pudding boiled with coconut. Vegetables play a significant role in the creation of Thai desserts as well, such as golden sweet potato or yam in a pudding, water chestnuts sliced into coconut cream, sago or tapioca in lime or coconut puddings, corn in coconut ice cream, mung beans in a sweet coconut syrup.

*Khanom*, "cake" or "small bite" in Thai, describes many of the elaborately crafted little sweetmeats eaten in Thailand and served to guests in the home. They go by delightful names like Thai silk (*foi tong*), golden threads of egg cooked in sugar syrup, and three chums (*sam kloe*). Most artistic of them all is mock marzipan fruit (*loog choob*), miniature fruits fashioned from mung-bean dough dipped into colored gelatin. Most of these are too difficult to prepare at home, which is not the case for the four desserts I have selected for this book.

# SWEET POTATO CUSTARD

FOR AUTHENTICITY, GARNISH THIS VEGETABLE BASED DESSERT WITH CARAMELIZED ONION. TO PREPARE THE ONION, FINELY SLICE 1 LARGE YELLOW ONION (ABOUT 1½ CUPS) AND GENTLY FRY IT OVER MEDIUM HEAT IN 4 TO 5 TEASPOONS VEGETABLE OIL OR BUTTER UNTIL CARAMELIZED TO A DEEP GOLDEN BROWN. IT WILL TAKE SOME TIME, AND REQUIRES YOUR CLOSE ATTENTION AT THE END TO MAKE SURE IT DOES NOT BURN. SPREAD ON PAPER TOWELS TO COOL AND CRISP. WHEN THE CUSTARD IS COOKED, REMOVE IT FROM THE OVEN AND SPREAD THE ONIONS EVENLY OVER THE TOP, THEN LEAVE TO COOL.

To make the custard, place the sweet potato on a steamer rack over simmering water, cover the steamer, and steam until tender, 6 to 8 minutes.

Meanwhile, preheat an oven to 350 degrees F. Spray an 8-by-6-by-1½-inch cake pan or heatproof serving dish with nonstick cooking spray, or grease with butter or vegetable oil. Set aside.

Remove the sweet potato from the steamer and place in a food processor. Process until smooth, then wait for a few minutes for the sweet potato to cool. Add the eggs, coconut cream, salt, sugar, and vanilla and process again until smooth and creamy. Strain through a sieve into the prepared pan and set the pan inside a larger baking pan. Add warm water to the baking pan to reach halfway up the sides of the custard dish.

Bake until a skewer inserted in the center comes out clean, about 45 minutes. Remove from the oven and set on a rack to cool.

To prepare the coconut cream, in a small saucepan over medium-low heat, combine the coconut cream and salt. Bring to a simmer and cook until it has thickened and slightly caramelized, about 15 minutes.

To make the palm sugar syrup, in another saucepan mix together the sugar and water. Place over low heat and simmer, stirring to dissolve the sugar, until syrupy, about 12 minutes.

Serve the custard and its accompaniments warm or cold. Cover the custard with the caramelized onion, if using (see introduction). Cut the custard into squares, place on individual plates, and form pools of the syrup and the coconut cream on each plate.

For the Custard

1¼ cups (7½ ounces) cubed golden
    sweet potato

3 eggs

¾ cup coconut cream

¼ teaspoon salt

1 tablespoon superfine white sugar

1 teaspoon vanilla extract

For the Coconut Cream

1½ cups coconut cream

Big pinch of salt

For the Syrup

1 cup (5 to 5½ ounces) dark palm
    sugar or dark brown sugar

½ cup water

# COCONUT RICE PUDDING

ROASTED PEANUTS AND CRUSHED GINGER OR HONEY COOKIES GIVE THIS RICE PUDDING ADDED APPEAL, BUT IT IS THE BUTTERSCOTCH SAUCE THAT TURNS THE SIMPLE INTO THE SENSATIONAL. BOTH PUDDING AND SAUCE CAN BE MADE AHEAD AND REHEATED IN A MICROWAVE OVEN. ALTHOUGH THERE ARE SEVERAL STEPS TO THIS RECIPE, THEY ARE ACTUALLY QUITE SIMPLE TO DO.

To make the pudding, rinse the rice several times, then place in a bowl, add water to cover, and let stand for 1 hour. Drain and place in a heatproof dish that will fit inside your steamer. It should be about 8 inches square and 2 inches deep. Add the coconut milk, salt, dried coconut, and sugar; stir well. Pour about 2 inches of water into the bottom of the steamer and bring to a boil. Reduce the heat so the water simmers, and place the pudding on the rack over the water. Cover and steam until the pudding is thick, about 30 minutes. Add hot water as needed to maintain the original level in the steamer pot.

Meanwhile, make the coconut custard. In a bowl, beat together the coconut cream, eggs, and vanilla until well blended. Pour the mixture evenly over the partially cooked rice pudding. Re-cover the steamer and cook the pudding 15 to 20 minutes longer. The total cooking time is 45 to 50 minutes.

While the pudding is steaming, make the sauce: In a small nonreactive saucepan combine the palm sugar and coconut cream and bring to a simmer over medium heat. Cook until syrupy, about 7 minutes. Add the vanilla and then whisk in the butter. In a small bowl, mix together the cornstarch and water and stir into the sauce. Cook, stirring slowly, until the sauce thickens, about 2 minutes. Remove from the heat and set aside.

To make the crust, place the peanuts and broken-up cookies or sesame seeds in a food processor or blender. Chop to the consistency of coarse crumbs.

When the pudding is ready, spread the mixed peanuts and cookies (or sesame seeds) evenly over the pudding and allow to sit for a minute or so, then cut into squares to serve. Place each serving onto a plate and pour on a generous quantity of the butterscotch sauce. Serve the pudding and sauce warm or cold.

¾ cup long-grain white glutinous rice

2¼ cups coconut milk

½ teaspoon salt

⅓ cup shredded dried coconut

⅓ cup superfine white sugar

1 cup coconut cream

2 medium eggs

½ teaspoon vanilla extract

1 cup dark palm sugar or dark brown sugar

½ cup coconut cream

1 teaspoon vanilla extract

½ cup butter, at room temperature, cut into pieces

3 to 4 teaspoons cornstarch

2 tablespoons water

⅓ cup (2 ounces) unsalted roasted peanuts

2 gingersnaps or other crisp, honey- or ginger-flavored cookies, or 1 tablespoon toasted sesame seeds

# LIME SAGO PUDDING

SERVES 4 TO 6

SAGO AND TAPIOCA ARE USED IN MANY POPULAR ASIAN DESSERTS. BOTH ARE A BLAND-FLAVORED STARCH PRODUCT FORMED INTO A SMALL, WHITE BALL. SAGO IS THE SIZE OF SEED PEARLS, WHILE TAPIOCA IS LARGER, THE SIZE OF SMALL GREEN PEAS. THEIR TASTE IS SIMILAR, AND THEY CAN BE USED INTERCHANGABLY IN RECIPES. WHEN COOKED, THEY TURN TRANSLUCENT. THIS IS A SIMPLE AND REFRESHING SWEET ON ITS OWN. SERVED WITH A BOUQUET OF ATTRACTIVELY SLICED TROPICAL FRUITS, AS THEY DO IN THAILAND, AND A DRIZZLE OF COCONUT CREAM, THIS PUDDING BECOMES AN IMPRESSIVE END TO A MEAL.

1½ cups sago (see introduction)

5 cups water

½ teaspoon salt

5 fresh kaffir lime leaves, or 1 tablespoon finely shredded lime zest

½ cup granulated white sugar

1 to 3 tablespoons freshly squeezed lime juice

For the Coconut Cream

1½ cups coconut cream

Big pinch of salt

2 to 4 cups sliced ripe fruits- such as star fruit (carambola), mango, papaya, peach, or nectarine, in any combination

In a nonreactive saucepan, combine the sago, water, and salt and bring to a boil over high heat, stirring continuously. Reduce the heat to medium and simmer, stirring frequently, for about 10 minutes. Lightly crush 4 of the lime leaves and add to the pan with the sugar. If you plan to use the lime zest instead, do not add it at this stage.

Continue to simmer the sago until cooked, about 5 minutes. It will be translucent, and with no white specks showing. Add the lime zest, if using, and lime juice, making it as tart as you prefer. (I usually use the juice of 2 medium-sized limes.) Rinse 4 to 6 small molds or dessert dishes with water and divide the sago evenly among them. Set aside to cool and firm up, then chill well.

If using kaffir lime leaves, fold the remaining leaf in half lengthwise, cut away the tough central rib with a small, sharp knife, and shred the leaf very finely. Set aside.

To prepare the coconut cream, in a small saucepan over medium-low heat, combine the coconut cream and the salt. Bring to a simmer and cook until it has thickened and slightly caramelized, about 15 minutes. Remove from the heat and let cool to room temperature.

When ready to serve, run a wet knife around the inside edge of each pudding mold or dish and invert onto chilled individual plates. Sprinkle the lime leaf shreds over the top, if using, and surround with the fruits and a pool of coconut cream.

# BANANAS IN COCONUT MILK

SERVES 4 TO 6

**T**HIS IS ONE OF THE EASIEST DESSERTS IMAGINABLE, AND IT IS PARTICULARLY ENJOYABLE SERVED WARM ON A COLD NIGHT. I LIKE TO USE A SWEETER BANANA VARIETY, BUT YOU MAY HAVE YOUR OWN PREFERENCE. THINNER, LESS RICH COCONUT MILK CAN BE USED IN PLACE OF THE COCONUT CREAM.

2⅓ cups coconut cream

⅓ cup light palm sugar or raw or light
    brown sugar

1 teaspoon salt

4 bananas

2 tablespoons cornstarch

½ cup (1½ ounces) shredded dried
    coconut

Pour the coconut cream into a nonreactive saucepan and add the sugar and salt. Bring almost to a boil, stirring to dissolve the sugar. Reduce the heat so the coconut cream continues to simmer.

Peel and thickly slice the bananas crosswise. Coat the slices with the cornstarch, shaking off the excess. Add the bananas to the coconut cream and cook for about 4 minutes, then turn off the heat and allow them to sit in the hot coconut cream for at least 10 minutes if serving them warm. Or allow to cool, then chill in the refrigerator to serve cold.

Spread the coconut in a small skillet without oil. Cook over medium-low heat, shaking the pan and stirring continuously so the coconut cooks evenly, until golden brown. Remove from the heat.

Spoon the bananas and their sauce into bowls and add a big pinch of toasted coconut to each serving.

# INDEX

# TABLE OF EQUIVALENTS

THE EXACT EQUIVALENTS IN THE FOLLOWING TABLES HAVE

BEEN ROUNDED FOR CONVENIENCE.

## US/UK

oz = ounce
lb = pound
in = inch
ft = foot
tbl = tablespoon
fl oz = fluid ounce
qt = quart

## METRIC

g = gram
kg = kilogram
mm = millimeter
cm = centimeter
ml = milliliter
l = liter

## WEIGHTS

| US/UK | Metric |
|---|---|
| 1 oz | 30 g |
| 2 oz | 60 g |
| 3 oz | 90 g |
| 4 oz (¼ lb) | 125 g |
| 5 oz (⅓ lb) | 155 g |
| 6 oz | 185 g |
| 7 oz | 220 g |
| 8 oz (½ lb) | 250 g |
| 10 oz | 315 g |
| 12 oz (¾ lb) | 375 g |
| 14 oz | 440 g |
| 16 oz (1 lb) | 500 g |
| 1½ lb | 750 g |
| 2 lb | 1 kg |
| 3 lb | 1.5 kg |

## OVEN TEMPERATURES

| Fahrenheit | Celsius | Gas |
|---|---|---|
| 250 | 120 | ½ |
| 275 | 140 | 1 |
| 300 | 150 | 2 |
| 325 | 160 | 3 |
| 350 | 180 | 4 |
| 375 | 190 | 5 |
| 400 | 200 | 6 |
| 425 | 220 | 7 |
| 450 | 230 | 8 |
| 475 | 240 | 9 |
| 500 | 260 | 10 |

## LIQUIDS

| US | Metric | UK |
|---|---|---|
| 2 tbl | 30 ml | 1 fl oz |
| ¼ cup | 60 ml | 2 fl oz |
| ⅓ cup | 80 ml | 3 fl oz |
| ½ cup | 125 ml | 4 fl oz |
| ⅔ cup | 160 ml | 5 fl oz |
| ¾ cup | 180 ml | 6 fl oz |
| 1 cup | 250 ml | 8 fl oz |
| 1½ cups | 75 ml | 12 fl oz |
| 2 cups | 500 ml | 16 fl oz |
| 4 cups/1 qt | 1 l | 32 fl oz |

## LENGTH MEASURES

| | |
|---|---|
| ⅛ in | 3 mm |
| ¼ in | 6 mm |
| ½ in | 12 mm |
| 1 in | 2.5 cm |
| 2 in | 5 cm |
| 3 in | 7.5 cm |
| 4 in | 10 cm |
| 5 in | 13 cm |
| 6 in | 15 cm |
| 7 in | 18 cm |
| 8 in | 20 cm |
| 9 in | 23 cm |
| 10 in | 25 cm |
| 11 in | 28 cm |
| 12 in/1 ft | 30 cm |